D0607623

Dedicated to the women in my life

Cauliflower

Over 70 Exciting Ways to Roast, Rice, and Fry
One of the World's Healthiest Vegetables

....
Oz Telem
....

hardie grant books

Preface:
Welcome to my first cookbook

When people ask me what exactly do I do for a living, my reply is, 'I help spread happiness through cooking.' This is the ultimate goal of every post I publish on my blog – thekitchencoach.co.il – and every article I write.

Whenever you prepare a successful dish at home – one that makes you and your loved ones smile – you create joyful moments and pleasant, happy memories. It is a great privilege for me to be the person whose words help forge such moments.

I am excited to learn and discover the potential of humble ingredients, such as cauliflower, and convey that knowledge to other people.

Why cauliflower?

The idea of dedicating an entire book to 'the white princess' came from my wife, Adi. Once she suggested the idea, it was like a lightbulb switched on. It felt so right, I knew I could devote myself wholeheartedly to this subject.

Of course, everyone loves cauliflower. It is nutritious and delicious, easy to find and can be cooked in every possible way. Yet, when I asked around, I found that most people knew only three or four ways to prepare it. So, I saw a gap I could fill.

In my research for the book, I collected recipes from Israel and abroad, from family and friends, and from readers who heard about my project. Many dishes borrow techniques usually reserved for other ingredients.

Another great source of inspiration was the internet. Many wonderful cauliflower ideas are trending online, and between the pages you'll find my take on those I liked the most. You will also find recipes and methods that I developed from scratch and that feature here for the first time.

Before you start cooking

All the recipes were written for and tested by home cooks. I have put great thought into writing the cooking steps, as they are the building blocks of a succesful dish.

In almost every recipe you will find tips and instructions on how to make the dish gluten-free, vegan and even paleo-friendly.

If you are cooking the gluten-free recipes, remember that traces of gluten might be found in spices, nuts, bottled sauces and more, so shop with extra care.

I am at your service for any questions that might arise while using the book, so contact me at: Oz@thekitchencoach.co.il and don't forget to follow my Instagram @oztelem and tag #caulibook whenever you are cooking from the book!

Contents

Introduction to cauliflower

Blooming history

The star ingredient of this book belongs to a well-established family, the Brassicaceae, with many of its members considered superfoods, as they are packed with nutritional value. The 'father' of the cauliflower is a plant called wild cabbage (*Brassica oleracea*), that still grows wild in some parts of the Mediterranean and Western Europe. Wild cabbage is the ancestor of many commonly loved vegetables.

Farmers started cultivating it around 4,000 years ago, and through the years, breeds with distinct characteristics emerged. A cultivar with a dense head of leaves became cabbage; one with a swollen stem became kohlrabi and another with concentrated green florets became known as broccoli.

Some wild cabbage varieties concentrated their buds to form small heads – and ancient growers found them to be delectable. They kept and used the seeds from that mutation, and thanks to them we have cauliflower. Where exactly did the first white floret emerge? It is unclear. Some historic evidence points towards ancient Rome, others to medieval Syria and Turkey. Wherever it originated, today it is grown worldwide.

Lady cabbage

In almost every Latin language, the meaning of the name cauliflower is flowering cabbage. 'Cauli' is an old word for cabbage. Its Hebrew name is *kroovit*, which translates to 'lady or female cabbage' since, in Hebrew, all nouns are treated linguistically in male or female forms. That's why the cauliflower is the queen of vegetables.

Exposure to light

Broccoli is grown exposed to the sun, thus developing a green colour (thanks to the pigment chlorophyll). However, cauliflower gets no tanning time: it is grown covered and wrapped in its outer leaves, which , in turn, protect it from the sun, allowing it to develop and accumulate the white buds we know and love.

Once a cauliflower is exposed to direct sunlight, it takes on purple and yellow hues and goes into blossoming mode, which greatly shortens its shelf life.

From sprout to full head, it takes about three months (depending on season and variety) for cauliflower to reach harvest size. Though it is available year-round, the most pristine heads grow during winter and spring.

Giant heads

According to Meir Machluf, one of the most prolific growers of cauliflower in Israel, its optimal harvest weight is around 1.2 kg (2.6 lb) per head.

In this book, when a medium-sized cauliflower is referred to, it should weigh about 1 kg (2 lb 3 oz). Cauliflower heads can greatly exceed this size, and grow to over 3 kg (6 lb 9 oz) in weight, but farmers rarely let them grow this large because of a lack of demand.

However, if you stumble upon an extra-large cauliflower, know that it can deliver great value for the money. I once stretched a 2½ kg (5 lb 8 oz) cauliflower to four different dishes, and it cost mere pennies at the local market.

How to select

Turn the cauliflower upside down and look at its central main stem. It should look as though it was just cut from the plant: moist, not dry or cracked. The florets should be tight-fitting and firm to the touch, preferably free of any blemished areas. Note that the florets bruise easily, and sellers might trim away those bits (and that's OK).

If the leaves and stalks surrounding the cauliflower are nice and fresh, tell your greengrocer to keep them on – you will find many uses for them in the following pages.

small cauliflower
700–800 g
(1 lb 8oz–1 lb 12 oz)

medium cauliflower
1–1.2 kg
(2 lb 3 oz–2 lb 10 oz)

large cauliflower
2 kg
(4 lb 7 oz) and up

How to store

Cover the florets with paper towel (if it came covered in cling film (plastic wrap), remove it). Place in a paper bag and stash in the bottom of the fridge, where it will keep for up to a week (depending on how fresh it was when bought).

How to freeze

Any excess cauliflower you might end up with after you have cooked your main recipe can be stored in the freezer for future use. Florets should be cut to a similar size (see page 18) and kept in resealable bags for easy access.

Using defrosted florets is similar to using pre-cooked ones: they lack the crunch and freshness needed for raw salads, but otherwise, they can be used in almost any other preparation.

How to clean

Particularly during summertime, cauliflower might attract several species of insects. For thorough cleaning, break the cauliflower into small florets, then soak in cold water with a teaspoon of salt and a tablespoon of distilled vinegar. Leave the florets to sit for 10 minutes, then rinse.

Nutritional value

The cauliflower is a bud, the part that would eventually be responsible for future generations. It is a staple in various detox diets, as it is a good source of potassium, folic acid, vitamins C and K, carbohydrates and several types of proteins (like amino acids). These proteins and carbohydrates are responsible for the cauliflowers unique ability to become attractively golden when roasted or fried (see pages 25 and 29).

The elephant in the room

As when consuming beans and Jerusalem artichoke, there are side-effects to enjoying cauliflower. It contains a complex carbohydrate named mannitol, which cannot be digested by our small intestine. It passes through the digestive track to the large intestine, where it is ravenously eaten by hungry microbes, which release ... gas. That is why people suffering from IBS abstain from cauliflower, as well as breastfeeding mothers (mannitol passes through milk to the baby).

Some claim that prolonged cooking may reduce the symptoms, others claim that consuming caraway and cumin before having cauliflower also helps.

Fractals all around

When you cut an onion or a pepper, you create cubes. However, when you cut cauliflower, each floret is identical in shape to that of the entire head. This natural pattern, of a shape that is composed of smaller shapes repeating themselves, is called a fractal. It is common in flowers, various cacti, and even cabbage heads are considered fractals.

Pearly white

The pigment responsible for the cauliflower's pearly white colour is called anthoxanthin, which is also responsible for the pale colours of potatoes and onions. It is a water-soluble (rather than oil-based) pigment that leaches out whenever cooked in water.

When you cook cauliflower with no water (for example when oven-roasting, see page 76) – the colour is retained, but it will be less tender. When lightly cooked, the cauliflower rapidly takes on the colour of more powerful pigments, like the ones found in beetroot and turmeric (see pages 52–53).

Cauliflower cuts

Whenever you pick up a cauliflower at the market, you are welcoming not one, but four different vegetables into your home. Aside from the prime cut of the florets, each part of the cauliflower has its own distinct use.

During summer the following parts are less attractive, and rarely even make it to the stores, but during the rest of the year they should not be discarded. Maximising the use of the whole cauliflower and its parts will help you get better value for your money and help reduce food waste.

Leaves

Slightly bitter, sturdy greens, that are very similar to kale (genetically, nutritiously and culinary), cauliflower leaves must be cooked until they are tender. They lend an earthy bitterness to various dishes and can be braised (see page 202), stuffed (like vine leaves) and also oven-roasted (like kale chips).

Main stem

The thick stem that holds the head is the culinary equivalent of kohlrabi: once you peel away the fibrous outer layer, you have a root-like vegetable that can be cut into matchsticks and added to crispy salads (see page 44) or oven-roasted like Jerusalem artichokes. The stem is also useful when added to cauliflower mash or cream (see page 32), taking full advantage of an otherwise neglected part.

Stalks

Through each of the leaves surrounding the head of cauliflower, runs a thick central vein that carries sugars to the plant and water to the leaves. We shall refer to them as stalks, as they play a similar role to other edible stalks, like those of celery and fennel.

Full of flavour and texture, they can be chopped and added to any recipe that calls for celery, like soups, stews and rices (see paella, page 218 and *maqluba*, page 210). If the stalks are nice and fresh, they can even be chopped, oven-roasted and added to your next antipasti platter.

Cauliflower varieties

Other than your classic white, farmers now grow a rainbow of caulis: yellow, orange, green and purple. Don't be shy about using them: they cook in the same way and might even offer a more intricate flavour. However, do try to use them in recipes that show off their shape and colour – don't just throw them into a mash.

Romanesco

The uniquely-shaped romanesco is eye-catching for sure. Thought to have originated in 16th century Italy, it is available during the cooler months of the year.

Slightly firmer than broccoli and cauliflower (yet really quite similar to them in flavour), romanesco takes a little more time to cook. Try using it instead of cauliflower in the pasta ragu (see page 156), and the gnocchi (see page 162) or turn it into popcorn (see page 76).

Basic preparation and cooking techniques

Prime cut: florets
How to cut cauliflower into florets

The easiest way to turn a head of cauliflower into manageable florets is to place it upside down on a cutting board, with the main stem facing you. Using a sharp paring knife, or a small serrated knife, run the blade around the main stem, cutting through the minor stems, and the florets will fall off. The remaining florets from the top of the head can be harvested similarly.

The florets from the base of the cauliflower tend to be larger than those at the top, so it is important to trim them to a uniform size. Throughout the book I have used a few different shapes and sizes of florets for you to utilise. To clarify:

Bite size – florets the size of a whole walnut, that you can finish in a bite or two

Medium size – larger than bite size

Large florets – florets harvested and not trimmed down

If your cauliflower has yielded too many florets, you can store them in the fridge for up to a day (they tend to oxidise at the cut end), or freeze in an airtight container for up to three months. Once defrosted, the florets will be more tender, ready to be cooked, baked or fried.

bite size

medium size

large florets

Cauliflower 'grains'
Good things happen when you grate cauliflower

The most exciting culinary development in the history of the cauliflower has occurred in recent years, when home cooks (and chefs) unlocked the vast potential of finely chopped or grated cauliflower. Cauliflower 'grains', if you will (or crumbs, though they are not crispy when cooked). Their delicate crumbly texture allows them to stand in for bulgur wheat, rice and couscous, the perfect substitute for anyone who seeks to cut down on carbs.

When raw, the 'grains' oxidise quite rapidly, and are best served the day you make them. You can also create large batches, divide and freeze in resealable bags for up to three months. Once defrosted, the grains will be softer, like steamed cauliflower couscous (see page 24).

There are three ways to transform the florets into grains:
1. Pulsing the florets 5–7 times in the food processor yields fine textured uniformly sized grains/ crumbs, suitable for couscous or cauliflower pizza crust (see page 170).

2. Using a box grater: rice-like texture
    Grating florets in a box grater, yields a variety of shapes and sizes, some very similar to that of rice. Use the grating attachment of your food processor to speed things up.

3. Hand chopping: funky random texture
    Hand chopping the cauliflower (using a sharp knife) yields uneven grains/crumbs. With this lack of uniformity, every bite you take feels slightly different than the other, and that's what makes dishes like linguine with cauliflower ragu (see page 156) so fun to eat.

knife

box grater

food
processor

Cauliflower stock
Using the leftovers

Many home cooks don't make their own stock but there is nothing to be afraid of – in fact, it is no more than making tea, only the flavour comes from vegetables or bones instead of dried leaves. You can use your stock as a base for soups, sauces and various rice and grain dishes to impart more depth of flavour than if you just use water.

Cauliflower stock is the simplest way to utilise the underused parts from the body of the vegetable. Just put some roughly chopped stems, leaves and stalks – basically, everything but the florets – in a large saucepan, cover with water, bring to the boil, then simmer for about 30 minutes. You waste nothing and create a lovely homemade stock without spending anything on extra ingredients. If you ask your local greengrocer for any trimmings, you might get them free of charge – they usually go straight to the bin! What a horrible waste!

You can, of course, add other neglected veggie parts to your stock pan, such as broccoli stems, leek leaves (the green part), Swiss chard stalks, potato skins and more, adding even more flavour and minimising food waste. Herbs that are waiting in the fridge, like parsley, spring onions or celery leaves are also welcome to join the stock.

Whenever I use cauliflower, I keep the body (or leftover parts) in the freezer (my wife says it's like a cauliflower graveyard!) and once I have enough I fill up a large stock pot. I like freezing the prepared stock in small resealable bags or containers so it's ready to defrost when I need it.

makes 1½ litres (51 fl oz/6 cups) / vegan / prep and cook: 35 minutes

Ingredients
stems, leaves and stalks from 2-3 medium-sized cauliflowers, well rinsed
1½ litre (51 fl oz/6 cups) water
sea salt

Method
- Roughly chop the various parts of the cauliflower. Place in a medium-sized pot, cover with water, season with salt and bring to a boil over high heat.

- Cover the pot and simmer over medium heat for 20-40 minutes, until the colour of the water changes.

- Place a large colander over a large bowl. Pour in the contents of the pot. Using a potato masher, press the vegetables to squeeze out all the moisture from them. Discard (or eat) the cooked vegetables.

- Allow the liquid to cool down, then divide between resealable bags or small containers. The stock keeps for a week in the refrigerator and 6 months in the freezer.

Whole steamed cauliflower
Using the power of steam to tenderise cauliflower

Some recipes call for boiling a whole head of cauliflower in a saucepan full of water, but for me, that is not the best way to tenderise it. Once the cauliflower is added to the saucepan, the water needs some time to return to a simmer and the nutrients from the florets leach out into the water during the long cooking time. The same goes for blanching florets, although to a lesser extent.

My solution? Stand the cauliflower upright in the pan, like a tree. This is a technique I first developed for broccoli, and it works even better with the star of this book.

When you stand the cauliflower in a saucepan, you only need enough water to come up to about 4 cm (2½ in) to cook the entire head! Once the sauce pan is covered and the water comes to a boil, the heat from the vapour penetrates the florets, collapsing their cell walls and making them more tender. The main stem of the cauliflower also softens in the process (don't worry – it won't burn).

Throughout the book, steaming is used as the primary cooking method, and it can be the only method you use. For the simplest healthy snack or side dish, just season some steamed florets with salt, olive oil and a squeeze of lemon juice. You can also get creative with your seasonings, and use some sesame oil and a sprinkle of toasted sesame seeds, smoked paprika and a little crushed garlic.

It's important to note that you don't have to steam the cauliflower whole if you don't feel like it. You can simply rinse the cauliflower, then chop off the stem and leaves, placing them in the bottom of a saucepan, add enough water almost to cover, then add the florets on top. Bring the water to the boil, cover and let the steam power do its work. No fancy steamer needed.

serves 3–4 / vegan / prep and cook: 30 minutes

Ingredients
1 medium-size cauliflower
2–3 tablespoons olive oil
2 tablespoons fresh lemon juice
sea salt and freshly ground black pepper

Method
- Trim the base of the main stem of the cauliflower so that it stands upright.

- Place in a medium-size saucepan with a lid. Add water to a height of 4 cm (2½ in).

- Place over a high heat, bring to the boil and cover.

- Steam for about 18 minutes – depending on the recipe you're making – to completely tenderise the cauliflower.

- To serve, cut the cauliflower into florets (see page 18), season with the olive oil, lemon juice, salt and black pepper to taste.

Fried cauliflower
Ten tips for successful deep-frying

If I could fry without using oil, then I would deep-fry everything. No other cooking method can deliver the golden brown colour, the lingering crispness and juicy textures achieved by a bath of hot oil.

The star of our book walks into the fryer in several recipes – sometimes coated in a batter, other times not. Here are ten tips that will help you become an expert fryer, then you can try out some of the fried cauliflower recipes in the book, such as Fried cauliflower with tahini and orange (see page 38).

My tips for the best golden-brown results:

· **Quality of the oil:** It is best to use unrefined oils, such as olive oil (not expensive extra-virgin) or grapeseed oil.

· **The right saucepan:** Use a thick, heavy-based saucepan that conducts heat slowly and evenly, and helps retain the temperature of the oil once you start frying.

· **Quantity of oil:** This might sound counter-intuitive, but the more oil you use, the better: smaller amounts of oil require more time to recover their temperature once the frying begins. Longer recovery means longer frying time – and the longer you fry, the more oil is absorbed into the food.

· **Amount of food:** Fry in small batches to ensure fast and even browning.

· **Precision:** It is best to use an oil thermometer to achieve the right oil temperature. If you don't have one, dip a sprig of spring onion in the oil – when it sizzles you are ready to go!

· **Heat control:** It is important to be mindful of the frying process. If the food is bubbling too rapidly and making too much noise, decrease the heat. If you hear nothing and see little bubbling, increase the heat.

· **Smoke:** If the oil begins to smoke before the frying action starts, it is too hot. Add a little cold oil to reduce the heat.

· **Fresh or steamed:** You can fry fresh florets or steamed ones, whichever you prefer. There's no right or wrong.

· **Use a slotted spoon:** It is easiest to remove the food from the oil using a spider or a slotted metal spoon. Transfer to a plate lined with kitchen paper towel to absorb any excess oil.

· **Reheating:** To warm up yesterday's fried foods, place them in a hot oven or toaster oven at 180°C (350°F/Gas 4) until crisp and hot right through.

Steamed cauliflower couscous
Lightly cooked cauliflower grains

I picked up this technique from chef Jamie Oliver, and it has been circling online for several years. The cauliflower grains are lightly cooked either in a pan or a microwave until they are tender and fluffy, and their texture resembles that of cooked rice or couscous.

Cauliflower couscous can serve as an accompaniment for soups and stews, take on Asian flavours and even become the base of a stir-fry (see page 138).

serves 2–4 (as a side) / vegan / prep and cook: 25 minutes

Ingredients
1 small cauliflower
sea salt

Method

- Cut the cauliflower into even-sized florets. Place in the bowl of a food processor and pulse 6–7 times until the cauliflower resembles the consistency of breadcrumbs. Alternatively, you can grate or chop the florets for a similar texture.

- **To cook in the microwave:** Put the cauliflower rice in a microwave-safe bowl and cover with a lid or microwave-safe cling film (plastic wrap). Microwave on high for 5 minutes until the grains are tender but not soft.

- **To cook in a saucepan:** Put the cauliflower rice in a medium-size saucepan (with no oil). Cover and cook over a high heat for 4–5 minutes, stirring occasionally, until tender and fluffy.

- Fluff with a fork and season with salt to taste.

Baked cauliflower florets
Oven-roasted until golden

When you place a cauliflower in the oven you surround it with dry heat that allows it to soften and become golden. For the perfect balance between a golden, slightly crisp, exterior and soft interior, I like to par-cook the florets by steaming them before roasting.

Baked florets can be served on their own in sandwiches (see page 74) or as a vegetable antipasto, and be part of more elaborate dishes, like a glorious cauliflower and pistachio quiche (see page 196).

serves 2–4 (as a side) / vegan / prep and cook: 40 minutes

Ingredients
1 medium-size cauliflower
3–5 tablespoons olive oil
sea salt

Method
- Preheat the oven to 190°C (375°F/Gas 5). Line a baking tray (baking sheet) with parchment paper.

- Steam the cauliflower whole (see page 24) for 10 minutes, or until just tender.

- Transfer to a large bowl, allow to cool slightly, then cut into medium-size florets. Roughly chop the main stem of the cauliflower.

- Add the oil and salt to the cauliflower and toss gently to coat.

- Spread the cauliflower on to the prepared baking tray and roast for 15–20 minutes until the florets are golden brown.

Caramelised cauliflower
Golden cauliflower grains

If there is one thing I would like to be remembered for, it is for making caramelised cauliflower into a thing people make and enjoy regularly. The idea came about after I made some cauliflower couscous and thought I'd take it up a notch.

I treated a batch of cauliflower grains the same way I would treat diced onions, and cooked them over a medium heat, in plenty of oil, until all the moisture had evaporated. This resulted in delicate, nutty, buttery flakes packed with the essence of cauliflower.

A fresh head of cauliflower contains about 5 per cent carbohydrates and 2 per cent protein, the majority of it being water. The water evaporates quickly when the small grains are cooked in oil.

Once most of the moisture has gone, the cauliflower begins to brown, thanks to a set of chemical reactions that occur when carbs and protein are exposed to temperatures over 110°C (230°F). Since a head of cauliflower yields only about a cup of caramelised cauliflower, it makes sense to make a large batch.

You can use caramelised cauliflower everywhere! Add some to creamy coconut sauces, homemade gnocchi, savoury porridge, polenta and bread puddings, burger patties, savoury scones – and that scarcely touches its potential.

Try replacing fried onions with caramelised cauliflower in rice dishes such as the rice and brown lentil mujadara (see page 204) or use it to impart a surprising flavour in savoury Parmesan cookies (see page 188).

makes about 180 ml (6½ fl oz/¾ cup) / vegan / prep and cook: 20–25 minutes

Ingredients
1 medium-size cauliflower
80 ml (3 fl oz/⅓ cup) olive oil
½ teaspoon sea salt

Method
· Cut the cauliflower into florets, then chop the florets finely to resemble breadcrumbs using a food processor, a box grater or a knife.

· Transfer to a wide pan, add the oil and salt, and cook over a medium-high heat, stirring frequently, for 12–16 minutes until golden. Make sure you don't overcook the grains – once golden, they will brown and burn quite quickly.

· Store the caramelised cauliflower for up to five days in the fridge or freeze for up to three months.

Cauliflower mash and cream
Silky smooth cauliflower purées

Here we have two types of cauliflower purée, both created in a very similar way – by cooking the florets in water, then blending – but differing in their consistency and therefore in their use.

Besides standing on its own as a soup, cauliflower cream can be used instead of double (heavy) cream in pasta sauces (see page 156) and in baked dishes such as sweet potato and potato gratin (see page 190). Cauliflower mash can substitute a classic potato mash as a side dish for hearty stews and casserole dishes, and serve as a flavourful, creamy substitute for béchamel and mashed potato in dishes like moussaka, lasagne and shepherd's pie.

Both mash and cream turn out silkier thanks to the addition of a fatty element: butter, double (heavy) or coconut cream and even olive oil. It is essential that you purée the florets while still hot, and that you keep the blender or food processor running for an extra 30 seconds after it seems done. The longer you purée, the smoother the finished result.

Your mash and cream will keep well in the fridge for up to four days. You may also freeze them (for up to three months). Once defrosted, they will no longer look smooth, so simply reheat and purée again to re-emulsify the mixtures.

serves 3–4 / vegan / prep and cook: 30 minutes

Ingredients
1 medium-size cauliflower
2 tablespoons butter or coconut oil
sea salt

Method
- Cut the cauliflower into florets, peel and roughly chop the main stem (reserving the stalks and leaves for making stock).

- Place the florets and stem in a medium-size saucepan. Add just enough water to cover the florets and bring to the boil over a high heat.

- Cook, uncovered, over a medium heat for 14–18 minutes, until the florets are fully tender and easily mashed with a fork.

To make the mash
- Strain the cauliflower and reserve the cooking liquid in a jug.

- If you are using a food processor, transfer the hot florets to the bowl, add the butter or oil and purée for 1 minute until very smooth, adding about 3–4 tablespoons of the cooking liquid, if necessary, to make a thinner mash (see opposite).

- If you are using a hand-held blender, return the hot florets the pan, add the butter or oil and purée thoroughly for about 2–3 minutes, adding about 3–4 tablespoons of the reserved liquid, if necessary, to make it easier to purée (see opposite).

- Season with salt to taste. Add a little of the reserved cooking liquid if you want a looser mash.

To make the cream

- Remove about 250 ml (9 fl oz/1 cup) of cooking liquid from the pan and set aside.

- If you are using a blender, transfer the hot florets and cooking liquid to the bowl, add the butter or oil and purée for 1 minute or until very smooth. Do this in batches if the blender bowl is not large enough (see above).

- If you are using a hand-held blender, add the butter or oil to the pan and purée for 2 minutes, or until very smooth (see above).

- Season with salt to taste. Add a little of the reserved liquid if you want a thinner cream.

Salads and pickles

Five-minute cauliflower tabbouleh
Carb-free

Tabbouleh is one of my all-time favourite salads. Packed with fresh, bright herbs, lemony tanginess, rich olive oil and bulgur wheat that absorbs all the flavours, which is replaced here with the cauliflower 'crumbs'. The salad was inspired by chef Yotam Ottolenghi, who has been advocating the benefits of cauliflower for years.

The cauli-crumbs provide the right texture and are a wonderful solution for the gluten intolerant and those who practise the paleo way of life.

My hack for making this salad even faster to make is pulsing the cauliflower and herbs together in a food processor. I got the idea during the crowd-funding campaign for the book. I was invited to one of Israel's live morning shows to promote the campaign. I woke up a little late, and barely had time to complete the five dishes I was supposed to present. Instead of hand chopping everything for the salad like I normally do, I just threw everything in the processor, and it worked amazingly well.

serves 3–4 / vegan / gluten-free / paleo /
prep and cook: 5 minutes

Ingredients

1 small cauliflower
about 120 g (4 oz/1 bunch) parsley, including stems
3–4 spring onions (scallions), both green and white parts
leaves from 10–20 mint sprigs (optional)
4–6 tablespoons olive oil
2–4 tablespoons freshly squeezed lemon juice (or more!)
sea salt and freshly ground black pepper

Method

1. Cut the cauliflower into medium-size florets (reserve the remaining parts for other uses). Roughly chop the parsley and spring onions.

2. Place the florets, parsley, spring onions and mint leaves, if using, in the bowl of a food processor. Pulse 5–7 times until the cauliflower resembles fine breadcrumbs and the herbs are finely chopped.

3. Empty the content of the food processor into a bowl. Season with olive oil, lemon juice and salt and pepper to taste. Serve at once.

Cauli**tip**

Feel free to add toasted chopped nuts (like almonds or pistachios) and dried cranberries or raisins to your tabbouleh party.

If you don't have a food processor, grate the cauliflower and finely chop the herbs.

Fried cauliflower with tahini and orange

A taste of the Galilee

When we travel to the Galilee, we like to eat at Sharabic, a wonderful, tiny restaurant owned by Ya'akub hi'yat, a true master of vegetables.

This chef serves what is, for me, the best fried cauliflower dish in Israel, which he pairs with dishes like charred aubergine (eggplant), wild berries, stuffed vine leaves and lemony okra (called ladies' fingers).

Like many chefs, Ya'akub adds smooth homemade tahini to his crispy fried florets, but his twist is what takes the dish to the next level: he squeezes unripe orange or mandarin juice on top, giving the dish a hit of acidity and tang. If you don't live next to an orchard, any sour fresh citrus you have available will work here (even lime and grapefruit).

For best results, make this dish on the day you buy the cauliflower; the fresher it is, the better it browns in the cooking oil.

If you are not in the mood for frying, you can bake your florets instead (see page 29).

serves 2–3 / vegan / gluten-free / prep and cook: 30 minutes

Ingredients

For the tahini

270 g (10 oz/1 cup) raw tahini (sesame seed paste)
250 ml (8½ fl oz/1 cup) cold water
2–4 tablespoons freshly squeezed lemon juice
fine sea salt, to taste

For the cauliflower

1 medium-size cauliflower
3–4 cups oil, for frying
1 sour orange or mandarin (preferably unripe)
sea salt, to taste

Method

1. **To prepare the tahini:** Place the raw tahini in a bowl, add 120 ml (4 fl oz/½ cup) of water and the lemon juice, and mix well to combine.

2. Gradually add more water until you have a smooth, pourable but not runny consistency. Season with salt and more lemon juice to taste.

3. **To cook the cauliflower:** Cut the cauliflower into bite-size florets (reserving the other parts for other uses).

4. Heat the oil in a medium-size, deep saucepan, using just enough oil to barely cover the florets.

5. Carefully add one-third of the florets and fry for 5–6 minutes until nicely golden and tender, moving the florets around in the oil using a slotted spoon for even browning.

6. Transfer the florets to a colander lined with kitchen paper and season with salt. Keep them warm while you fry the remaining florets in two batches.

7. Transfer the warm florets to serving plates. Add a couple of generous spoonfuls of the prepared tahini on top and squeeze some fresh orange over the tahini to finish.

Liat's salad
Black lentils with baked cauliflower, peppers and cashew nuts

I have a strong affinity for legume salads, especially for ones made with black lentils, which don't need soaking, are fast to cook, and are full of flavour and nutrients.

This is one of those salads you can make a day ahead and it will only improve. We got the recipe from Liat, a good friend of Noa's, the food stylist for the book. Liat is known as the salad champion, and likes preparing this colourful salad whenever she is entertaining at home.

The florets and peppers are baked together in the same pan. You can also bake and add the other parts of the cauliflower to the salad: peel the main stem and cut both the stem and the stalks to a similar size to that of the florets.

Feel free to add a small handful of raisins or dried cranberries, nuts (almonds and pine nuts, for example) and, of course, play around with different herbs: dill and mint would be great here. Add a teaspoon of vinegar (of your liking) for a more complex acidity.

For a dairy version, crumble some feta over the salad.

serves 4–5 / vegan / prep and cook: 1 hour

Ingredients

For the lentils

250 g (9 oz/1 cup) black or Puy lentils, well rinsed and drained
½ litre (20 fl oz/2½ cups) water
½ teaspoon sea salt

For the cauliflower and peppers

1 small cauliflower
2–3 red and/or yellow bell peppers, cut to 2–3 cm (1 in) cubes
2–3 tablespoons olive oil
½ teaspoon sea salt

For the salad

about 60 g (2½ oz/small bunch) parsley, chopped
1 small red onion, peeled and finely diced
60 g (2 oz/small handful) toasted cashew nuts, coarsely chopped
3–4 tablespoons olive oil
2–4 tablespoons freshly squeezed lemon juice
sea salt and freshly ground black pepper, to taste

Method

1. Preheat the oven to 190°C (375°F/Gas 5).

2. **For the lentils:** Place the lentils, water and salt in a medium-size saucepan. Bring to the boil over a high heat, partially cover and cook over a medium-low heat for 20–25 minutes until the lentils are tender, but not mushy, and all of the water has been absorbed. If the lentils are not soft enough, add some more hot water and continue to cook. Allow the lentils to cool.

3. **For the cauliflower and peppers:** Cut the cauliflower into bite-size florets, then place in a bowl with the diced peppers. Add the oil and salt, and toss to coat. Spread on a baking tray (baking sheet) lined with parchment paper and bake for 25–30 minutes until tender and golden. Allow the vegetables to cool down before adding them to the salad.

4. **To finish the salad:** Place the cooked lentils, peppers and cauliflower in a large mixing bowl. Add the parsley, onion and nuts. Season with oil, lemon juice and salt and pepper to taste. Mix well and serve.

Winter salad
Cauliflower with fennel, avocado and pomelo

Winter is the time of year I enjoy cooking the most. The markets are full of roots and bulbs, leafy greens are nice and vibrant and the cauliflower is at the peak of its beauty.

While shopping at the market preparation for the photo shoot of this book, I was inspired by all the beautiful citrus, just-ripe avocados and firm fennel. The produce was pleading to me to use it, so I went ahead with my intuition.

The photo shows purple and green cauliflower because it was on our set that day. If you can your hands get any colourful cauliflower, go ahead and use it in place of the regular one.

For the dressing, I use sumac, a tiny, dry and tangy fruit that grows in the mountains of Jerusalem (once used for leather-making), which adds an intriguing layer of acidity. If you can't get any ground sumac, use half a teaspoon of vinegar instead.

serves 2–3 / vegan / prep and cook: 1 hour

Ingredients
1 medium-size fennel bulb
½ small cauliflower
½ teaspoon sea salt
¼ large pomelo, peeled, pith removed
1 ripe avocado
30 g (1 oz/small handful) pumpkin seeds, toasted if you like

For the dressing
60 ml (2 fl oz/¼ cup) freshly squeezed orange juice
 or 2 tablespoons freshly squeezed lemon or lime juice
½ teaspoon ground sumac
3–4 tablespoons olive oil
sea salt and freshly ground black pepper

Method
1. Halve the fennel lengthways and slice thinly. Cut the cauliflower into small florets about the size of shelled walnuts. Peel and thinly slice the main stem.

2. Place the fennel and cauliflower in a bowl and add the salt. Mix well and set aside for 30 minutes until the vegetables have softened a bit.

3. Tear off the membrane and pull the pomelo segments into large pieces, transferring to a large bowl as you go. Halve the avocado, remove the stone and scoop out the flesh, then slice the flesh into 5 mm (¼ in) thick pieces and add to the pomelo.

4. Strain off any water in the bottom of the fennel and cauliflower bowl, then transfer the vegetables to the bowl with the pomelo. Add the pumpkin seeds.

5. Mix together the citrus juice, sumac and olive oil, drizzle over the salad and toss gently to coat. Add salt and pepper or citrus juice to taste. Serve at once.

Caulitip To toast the pumpkin seeds, place them in a dry pan over a medium heat. Toast for 2 minutes, stirring or shaking the pan, until the seeds emit a lovely nutty aroma.

Kohlrabi and apple slaw
Without kohlrabi

At the start of the book I declared that cauliflower stems are the culinary equivalent to kohlrabi. To prove that point, meet this salad, which is based on a traditional German recipe called *Kohlrabi mit Apfel* or: Kohlrabi with apple.

Instead of using it's next of kin, I used cauliflower stems, and even chefs who tasted the dish could not tell the difference.

Make sure you pick heads with nice thick stems, and tell your greengrocer not to trim them off. If you don't have enough stems for the salad (granted, it's not every day you purchase four heads), you can, of course add fine matchsticks of kohlrabi to add more volume.

Another well-known salad is referened here: celery and nuts are key components in Waldorf salad.

serves 2-3 / vegan / gluten-free / paleo / prep and cook: 20 minutes

Ingredients

4 cauliflower main stems
1 eating (dessert) apple, such as Granny Smith or Pink Lady
1–2 celery stalks with leaves
about 45 g (1½ oz/small handful) shelled pecan nuts

For the dressing

1 teaspoon apple cider or wine vinegar
1 tablespoon freshly squeezed lemon or lime juice
2–3 tablespoons olive oil
sea salt and freshly ground black pepper, to taste

Method

1. Peel the cauliflower stems (saving the fibrous outer layer for making stock). Cut each stem vertically into 2–3 pieces, then cut each piece into matchsticks.

2. Halve and core the apple, then cut to matchsticks. Thinly slice the celery stalks and finely chop the leaves. Roughly chop the nuts.

3. Put all the vegetables and apple in a mixing bowl. In a small bowl, mix together the vinegar, lemon or lime juice, oil, salt and pepper. Drizzle over the salad and toss to coat. Adjust the seasoning to taste.

4. Give the salad and final toss and serve. The salad can be prepared 2 hours in advance.

Caulitip

Replace the pecan nuts with other nuts; walnuts, toasted almonds and even hazelnuts work well.

Those who don't like raw celery can replace it with 30 g (1 oz/small handful) of freshly chopped parsley.

Cauliflower coucous salad
With leeks, peas and preserved lemon

Inspired by Jamie Oliver's filo rolls stuffed with couscous (real couscous), this warm salad follows a simple logic: if you can make steamed cauliflower couscous (see page 28), you can also make cauliflower couscous salad.

Here I recommend using a food processor to make the couscous. I find that grated and hand-chopped grains don't deliver the precise couscousy feel in the mouth.

Once hard to find, today you can buy preserved lemons in most good supermarkets and delis.

serves 3 / vegan / gluten-free / prep and cook: 30 minutes

Ingredients

1 small cauliflower
1 medium-size leek, well rinsed
2 tablespoons olive oil
about 90 g (3 oz/large handful) frozen peas
  (no need to defrost)
1 tablespoon finely chopped preserved lemons
  (from about 1–2 lemons) or 2–4 tablespoons freshly
  squeezed lemon juice
sea salt and freshly ground black pepper, to taste

Method

1. Cut the cauliflower into even-sized florets. Place in the bowl of a food processor and pulse 6–7 times until you reach a consistency similar to fine breadcrumbs.

2. Cut the leek into quarters lengthways, then thinly slice.

3. Heat the oil in a medium-size saucepan, add the leeks and sweat over a medium heat for 6–7 minutes, stirring occasionally, until slightly softened.

4. Add the peas and cauliflower crumbs and cook for 1 minute over a high heat, stirring continuously.

5. Turn off the heat, cover the pan and leave to rest 10 minutes until the peas are cooked and the cauliflower crumbs become tender.

6. Stir in the chopped preserved lemon or lemon juice, and season with salt and pepper to taste.

7. Serve warm or at room temperature.

Chopped fresh herbs, like dill or coriander, are a welcome addition to the salad, add them along with the lemon.

Caulitip

The leeks can be replaced with caramelised onions or baked bell peppers (see page 40).

Noa's Salad
Raw cauliflower with herbs and pomegranate

This recipe is by Noa Kanarek, the book's food stylist (see her on page 239 adorned with a cauli-hat). She says she created it by chance when she was looking for an easy, pretty dish to serve her family during the holiday season (that usually occurs in mid-September in Israel).

She chopped some lovely fresh cauliflower into small pieces, added some herbs, sunflower seeds and peanuts and bright red pomegranate seeds and, just like that, she had a winner.

Other nuts can be used for crunch: toasted and sliced almonds, chopped pecans, walnuts and pistachios all work wonderfully.

When fresh pomegranates are out of season, other seasonal fruit can be used instead: fresh raspberries, blackberries, strawberries and grapes all make great replacements.

serves 3–4 / vegan / gluten-free / prep and cook: 15 minutes

Ingredients

1 medium-size cauliflower
40 g (1½ oz/⅓ cup) sunflower seeds
50 g (2 oz/⅓ cup) toasted peanuts
  (see toasting instructions on page 50)
about 90 g (3 oz/1 small bunch) parsley, finely chopped
40 g (1½ oz/⅓ cup) dried blueberries, cranberries or raisins
seeds from 1 small pomegranate

For the dressing

2–3 tablespoons freshly squeezed lemon or lime juice
3–4 tablespoons olive oil
1 small garlic clove, minced (optional)
sea salt and freshly ground black pepper

Method

1. **For the dressing:** Place all the ingredients in a small bowl and whisk well with a fork. Season generously with salt and pepper.

2. Break the cauliflower into florets, then cut the florets into small pieces, about the size of peanuts, and put in a large mixing bowl.

3. Put the sunflower seeds in a dry pan and toast over a medium-low heat for about 3 minutes, stirring, until lightly golden. Add the seeds to the cauliflower.

4. Rub away the thin paper-like skins from the peanuts and roughly chop. Add them to the cauliflower with the parsley, blueberries and pomegranate seeds.

5. Pour over the dressing and toss together lightly. Taste and add more salt, oil or lemon juice to your liking.

6. Serve at once or cover with cling film (plastic wrap) and refrigerate for up to 2 hours before serving.

Caulitip Feel free to use other herbs (mint and/or basil will all work wonderfully here) and chopped spring onions (scallions).

Broccoli and cauliflower slaw
With mustard and peanuts

One of the most influential figures that helped shape the way I look at food is Alton Brown. His cooking show, *Good Eats*, placed a focus on ingredients, history, science and methods, rather than just recipes. Furthermore, it managed to do so while being entertaining and fun to watch.

In the epic episode 'If it ain't broccoli don't fix it' (series 11, episode 16), Brown deftly demonstrated how broccoli could be turned into a crunchy, cabbageless slaw.

Being a fan of *Game of Thrones*, I decided to unite the two siblings of the cruciferae banner into one salad. I even added another cruciferous member in the form of grainy mustard.

This salad travels well, making it ideal for picnics, and could be prepared a day in advance and kept in the fridge. Simply taste and re-season the salad after overnight refrigeration.

Like in Cauliflower Salad with Herbs and Pomegranate (see page 48), you can play around with the nuts and dried fruit you choose to add. Try pecans and raisins!

Serves 3–4 / vegan / prep and cook: 1½ hours

Ingredients

1 small cauliflower
1 head of broccoli (about the size of the cauliflower)
1 heaped teaspoon grain mustard
½ teaspoon sea salt (and more to taste)
½ teaspoon demerara or muscovado sugar (optional)
1 tablespoon apple cider or red or white wine vinegar
2 tablespoons freshly squeezed lemon or lime juice
2–3 tablespoons olive oil
35 g (1¼ oz/¼ cup) shelled peanuts, toasted
  (see toasting instructions in Cauli-tip)
30 g (1 oz/¼ cup) dried cranberries without added sugar

Method

1. Cut the cauliflower and broccoli into small florets, then slice thinly. Peel the main stems and thinly slice them too (reserve the remaining parts for other uses). Put all the slices in a large bowl.

2. Add the mustard, salt, sugar, vinegar and lemon or lime juice. Mix well to coat. Cover with cling film (plastic wrap) and chill for 1 hour until the vegetables are just tender.

3. Remove from the fridge. Add the oil, peanuts and dried cranberries. Taste and adjust the seasoning with more salt, lemon juice or sugar, and serve.

Caulitip

Another great addition to the salad is one eating (dessert) apple, such as a Granny Smith or Pink Lady, cored and cut to matchsticks, added with the oil.

To toast peanuts, lay them on a baking tray (baking sheet) lined with parchment paper. Toast in a preheated oven at 160°C (320°F/Gas 2) for 12 minutes or until golden. Allow to cool.

Starters and sides

Cauliflower steak
With spicy green herb salsa

Cauliflower steak was first created by American chef Dan Barber. He carves the thick, central cut of the cauliflower and treats it like a beef steak, searing it well on both sides. This sear brings out all the wonderful irresistible aromas locked inside the vegetable.

You can use the trimmed parts for any kind of mashed or puréed preparation, such as the cauliflower-coconut crown soup (see page 106) or cauliflower pasta alfredo (see page 158).

My recipe for this juicy cauliflower steak is served on a vibrant herb salsa – a kind of cross between Argentinian chimichurri and Spanish salsa verde with a spicy kick. Most salsas use vinegar or lemon juice, but I quite like their combination.

The salsa is great for almost any protein (from chicken to lamb) and is also wonderful on top of hummus.

serves 1–2 / vegan / prep and cook: 25 minutes

Ingredients
For the spicy green herb salsa
about 60 g (2 oz/½ bunch) parsley
about 60 g (2 oz/½ bunch) coriander (cilantro)
1 small green or red chilli, deseeded
 (you can put more or less to your liking)
1–2 garlic cloves, peeled and minced
1–2 tablespoons white wine vinegar
 (apple cider or red wine vinegar are also good)
1–2 tablespoons freshly squeezed lemon juice
5 tablespoons olive oil
fine sea salt and freshly ground black pepper
sugar, to taste (optional)

For the steak
1 small cauliflower
3 tablespoons olive oil
sea salt, to taste

Method
1. **To make the salsa:** Finely chop the herbs and chilli then place in a small bowl.

2. Add the garlic, vinegar, lemon juice and oil.

3. Season with salt and pepper, taste and if the salsa is too tangy, add some sugar to balance. You can also prepare the salsa by pulsing all the ingredients in a food processor to form a rough paste.

4. Store in a small jar in the fridge for up to a week.

5. **To cook the cauliflower steak:** Steam the cauliflower whole (see page 24) for 8–10 minutes until the main stem is slightly tender. Remove from the saucepan using a slotted spoon and let the cauliflower cool down a bit.

6. Lay the cauliflower upside down on a cutting board with the stem facing you. Trim off the sides of the cauliflower, leaving only the central cut, about 3–4 cm (1½ in) thick (see pictures overleaf). Use the trimmed parts for other dishes or munch them as you cook.

7. Heat a wide non-stick pan over a high heat. Liberally oil the cauliflower steak on all sides and season with salt.

8. Sear the cauliflower steak for 2–3 minutes on each side, until golden brown (see picture below).

9. Put 2–3 tablespoons of the prepared salsa on a serving plate. Lay the steak on top and serve.

Caulitip

When making 3–4 steaks or more, instead of steaming each cauliflower separately, cut into steaks and sear while raw, then lay on a baking tray (baking sheet) lined with parchment paper and bake at 180°C (350°F/Gas 4) until the main stem is tender.

If you don't like fresh coriander (cilantro), use only parsley for the salsa, increasing the quantity to one whole bunch. You can also add other herbs like chopped mint (leaves from 10 sprigs) and a couple of spring onions (scallions).

The steak also goes well with the lemon–butter sauce on page 70.

Whole roasted cauliflower
Minimalism at its best

This minimalist recipe takes a humble cauliflower and turns it into a glorious centrepiece. It is one of the most popular ways in Israel to prepare and serve the star of this book. A true showstopper as soon as it arrives at the table.

Whole roasted cauliflower was made famous in the US thanks to James Beard-awarded chef Alon Shaya, who pre-cooks his cauliflower in wine and spices, and serves it with whipped goats' cheese. It is also a signature dish of Israeli chef Eyal Shani, who serves it in his restaurants.

My take on the dish starts by steaming the cauliflower to partially soften its fibrous structure. Then it goes into the oven to roast, becoming excitingly crisp and golden outside and tender inside.

Be sure not to trim too many of the outer leaves and stalks – they become crisp in the oven.

serves 3–4 / vegan / gluten-free / paleo / prep and cook: 1 hour

Ingredients
1 medium-size cauliflower
3–4 tablespoons olive oil
fine sea salt and freshly ground black pepper

Method
1. Preheat the oven to 210°C (410°F/Gas 6).

2. Steam the cauliflower whole (see page 24) for 12–14 minutes until the florets are tender and the cauliflower is no longer pearly white in colour.

3. Remove from the saucepan using a slotted spoon and let the cauliflower cool down for about 10 minutes.

4. Transfer the cauliflower to a baking tray (baking sheet) lined with parchment paper. Drizzle the oil on top and massage the cauliflower so all the florets are oiled. Season generously with salt and pepper.

5. Roast in the oven for 20–30 minutes, or until golden brown all over and some bits are slightly charred.

6. Carefully transfer to a large serving plate and serve at once.

Béchamel Cauliflower
Baked whole

As part of my research for the book I looked through some old cookbooks to see if I could conjure up some arcane knowledge about our white princess. Many of these old books contained recipes for cauliflower baked in béchamel sauce – one of the five French mother sauces – which acts like a flavourful blanket to the cooked florets.

I wondered how I could add something new to this truly iconic dish, and the answer came from food writer and blogger Idit Narkis Katz, who suggested I keep the cauliflower whole rather than cut into florets.

Mustard (both in the sauce and the seeds sprinkled on top) adds a funky kick in terms of both flavour and texture. And before you ask: if you don't like (or don't have) mustard seeds, you can replace them with breadcrumbs.

Replace the butter with and equal amount of coconut oil and the milk with light coconut or soy milk for a vegan version and replace the flour with chickpea (gram) flour to make the dish gluten-free.

serves 3–4 / contains dairy / prep and cook: 1 hour

Ingredients

For the cauliflower
1 medium-size cauliflower
1 tablespoon yellow or black mustard seeds

For the béchamel sauce
30 g (1 oz/2 tablespoons) butter
1 heaped tablespoon plain (all-purpose) flour
480 ml (16 fl oz/2 cups) whole milk
1–2 tablespoons smooth Dijon or English mustard
sea salt, to taste

Method

1. Preheat the oven to 210°C (410°F/Gas 6).

2. **To cook the cauliflower**: Steam the cauliflower whole (see page 24) for 12–14 minutes until the florets are tender. Remove from the saucepan and let the cauliflower cool down a bit.

3. **To make the béchamel sauce**: Meanwhile, melt the butter in a medium-size saucepan over a high heat. Add the flour and stir vigorously for a few minutes until a thick paste forms. Reduce the heat to medium, add one-third of the milk and bring to the boil, stirring with a wooden spoon or whisk.

4. Add the remaining milk and return to the boil, still stirring. Simmer for 1–2 minutes over a medium-low heat until the sauce is thick enough to coat the back of a spoon. Remove from the heat, stir in the mustard and season with salt.

5. Transfer the cauliflower to a baking tray (baking sheet) with parchment paper. Pour the sauce over the top (see page 239) and sprinkle the top with mustard seeds. Roast for 18–22 minutes, until the béchamel becomes golden. Remove from the oven and serve at once.

Crispy baked breaded cauliflower
Maya's cauliflower

Maya is my wife, Adi's, younger sister. When she was a child she couldn't stand vegetables of any kind (except cucumbers). The first vegetable she agreed to eat was cauliflower that had been breaded and deep-fried like schnitzel. Today Maya calls many veggies her friends, and this crispy dish is still a favourite.

To create the same crispy effect without actually deep-frying, I charge ahead with two moves: first, I steam the cauliflower florets to tenderise them before sticking them in the oven. Second, I like to toast the breadcrumbs in a little oil, helping them brown up in the oven.

You can add a personal touch to any step of the breading process. For example, you can add some smooth or grainy mustard, sweet chilli sauce or smoked paprika to your beaten eggs, and jazz up the breadcrumbs with white or black sesame seeds.

Maya's mother and my mother-in-law, Yisra'ella, liked to add cinnamon and some crushed garlic to her beaten eggs.

serves 3–4 / contains egg / prep and cook: 45 minutes

Ingredients
1 medium-size cauliflower
2–3 tablespoons olive oil
50 g (2 oz/¾ cup) dried breadcrumbs, preferably panko
1 large egg, preferably free-range
sea salt and freshly ground black pepper

Method
1. Preheat the oven to 190°C (375°F/Gas 5) and line a baking tray (baking sheet) with parchment paper.

2. Steam the cauliflower whole (see page 26) for 7–9 minutes until the florets become slightly tender. Remove from the pan and let the cauliflower cool down a bit.

3. Cut the cauliflower into bite-size florets.

4. Add the breadcrumbs and oil to a wide pan and toast over a medium heat for 2–3 minutes, stirring, until the crumbs become slightly golden. Transfer to a shallow plate.

5. Crack the egg into a bowl, season with salt and pepper and beat well.

6. Dip the steamed florets into the beaten egg, then roll in the breadcrumbs until coated. Lay the breaded florets on the prepared baking tray .

7. Bake for 18–22 minutes until the breadcrumbs are nicely golden and crisp. Remove from the oven and serve, with condiments of your choice.

Caulitip

Vegan: Replace the egg, by beating together 3 scant tablespoons of chickpea (gram) flour with 4 tablespoons of water to form a batter.

Gluten-free: Replace the breadcrumbs with gluten-free cornflake crumbs.

Paleo: Replace the breadcrumbs with sesame seeds or crushed flaked (slivered) almonds.

Creamy cauliflower mash
With sautéed leeks

Recipes like this one are all over Pinterest. Here, the cauliflower plays the part of one of the most common vegetables on earth: the humble potato. Low on carbs and creamy in texture, kids go crazy over the cauli-mash as is.

This mash can be a side dish to any main course that would be served with mashed potatoes.

To give my mash more flavour, I added some garlic. You can, of course, omit it for a more neutral taste.

For texture, I topped the mash with sautéed leeks which add a nice bite. Typically, leeks are cooked for quite a long time – but if briefly cooked they retain some crunch. Many recipes call for discarding the green parts of the leeks. We like to use everything!

serves 3 / vegan / may contain dairy / gluten-free / paleo / prep and cook: 30 minutes

Ingredients

For the mash

1 medium-size cauliflower
3–6 large garlic cloves (optional), peeled and roughly chopped
30–60 g (1–2 oz/2–4 tablespoons) butter or coconut oil
sea salt, to taste

For the leeks

2–3 tablespoons olive oil
2 medium-size leeks, well rinsed and thinly sliced
  (both green and white parts)
sea salt, to taste

Method

1. **To make the mash:** Cut the cauliflower into florets, then peel and roughly chop the main stem (reserve the stalks and leaves for making stock, see page 22).

2. Place the cauliflower florets and stem, and garlic, if using, in a medium-size saucepan. Add enough water just to cover the florets, then bring to the boil over a high heat. Cook, uncovered, over a medium heat for 14–18 minutes until the florets are completely tender and easily mashed with a fork. Strain and reserve the cooking liquid.

3. Transfer the hot florets and garlic to the bowl of a food processor. Add the butter or oil and purée for 1 minute until very smooth, or use a hand-held blender (see page 32). Season the cauliflower mash with salt to taste and add some of the reserved cooking liquid for a thinner mash.

4. **To cook the leeks:** While the florets are cooking, heat a pan over a medium-high heat. Add the oil and sliced leeks and sauté, stirring frequently, for 6–8 minutes or until the leeks are just tender (you can cook it longer, but I like it a bit chewy). To speed up cooking, add 4 tablespoons of water. Season with salt to taste and set aside.

5. To serve, divide the mash between serving plates and top with the sautéed leeks.

Seared cauliflower with lemon butter
Inspired by the classic sole meunière

On the last night our of trip to Provence, Adi and I went exploring in the beachside town of Bandol. We came across a tiny restaurant run by a married couple where they were serving truly exceptional local dishes.

We ordered sole meunière, a classic French dish of delicately fried fish served with a lemony butter sauce. That splendid dish inspired this vegetarian starter.

I took green cauliflower and turned it into mini steaks. (for more contact area in the pan), and served them dipped in the sauce. You can, of course, use regular cauliflower, and broccoli also yielded good results when tested.

If you don't have access to naturally yellow butter, add ⅛ teaspoon of ground turmeric to give your sauce a delicate shade of yellow.

For a dairy-free version, you can replace the butter with 80 ml (3 fl oz/⅓ cup) full-fat coconut cream.

serves 2–3 / contains dairy / gluten-free / paleo / prep and cook: 20 minutes

Ingredients

For the lemon butter sauce

2–3 garlic cloves, peeled and minced or finely grated
2 tablespoons olive oil
2 tablespoons freshly squeezed lemon or lime juice
60 ml (2 fl oz/¼ cup) white wine
60 g (2 oz) good-quality butter, diced
fine sea salt, to taste

For the cauliflower

1 small cauliflower, preferably the green variety
3 tablespoons olive oil
leaves from 10 thyme sprigs, to garnish

Method

1. **To make the lemon butter:** Place the garlic in a small saucepan with the oil. Cook over a medium heat for 30–40 seconds until the garlic is fragrant, keeping a close eye on it so it doesn't burn.

2. Add the lemon or lime juice and wine, bring to the boil and simmer until reduced by two-thirds.

3. Turn off the heat and add the diced butter. Gently stir until the butter has melted and you have a smooth sauce. Season with salt and more lemon or lime juice, if you wish.

4. **To cook the cauliflower:** Cut the cauliflower into florets. Lay the florets on a cutting board, with the stems facing you, then trim the sides of the florets to form mini steaks (see page 58), about 1 cm (½ in) thick (thick mini steaks should be halved lengthways).

5. Heat the oil in a wide pan over a high heat. Add one layer of the cauliflower slices and sear for 2 minutes on each side until golden. Remove to a plate and repeat with the remaining slices.

6. To serve, divide the lemon butter between serving plates. Lay the seared cauliflower on top and garnish with thyme.

Crispy pitta with feta and cauliflower
Inspired by the Arab Ara'yes

One popular street food to search for when travelling to the market of Nazareth in Israel is called *Ara'yes*, or *arusa* (depending on who you ask). This ingenious dish is a kebab of freshly minced meat, herbs and spices, which is grilled in a pitta bread. The bread turns crisp and absorbes all the juices.

I had a vision of creating a *cauli-ra'yes*, and that vision was successfully fulfilled (we were all drooling on set while Assaf and Noa were working on the photo). I took baked cauliflower florets, chopped them up and mixed them with feta cheese and herbs for a surprisingly simple yet satisfying pitta filling.

If you can't find any good-quality pittas, you can replace them with tortillas and use the filling to make quesadillas instead.

Those who do not eat dairy products can replace the feta with 150 g (5 oz, ½ cup) of silken tofu, mashed together with 1 teaspoon of miso paste and ½ teaspoon of vinegar.

serves 3 / contains dairy / prep and cook: 40 minutes

Ingredients

For the filling

1 small cauliflower
2–3 tablespoons olive oil
150 g (5 oz/1 cup) crumbled full-fat feta cheese
1 spring onion (scallion), finely chopped
15 g (1/2 oz/small handful) parsley, finely chopped
1/2 teaspoon ground sumac (optional)
sea salt and freshly ground black pepper

For the pittas

3 pitta breads
3 tablespoons olive oil
fresh vegetables, to serve

Method

1. Preheat the oven to 190°C (375°F/Gas 5) and line a baking tray (baking sheet) with parchment paper.

2. **To make the filling:** Steam the cauliflower whole (see page 24) for 10 minutes, or until just tender. Drain and then transfer to a cutting board, then cut into medium-size florets. Roughly chop the main stem of the cauliflower.

3. Place the florets and stem in a large bowl, add the oil and season lightly with salt then toss to coat. Lay the cauliflower on the prepared sheet. Bake for about 15–20 minutes until the florets are golden. Remove and allow to cool slightly. Keep the oven on and don't discard the paper.

4. Chop the baked cauliflower into small pieces and put in a bowl. Add the feta, spring onion, parsley and sumac, if using. Stir to combine the ingredients.

5. **To fill the pitta breads:** Halve the pitta horizontally and fill each pocket with the filling mixture.

6. Heat the oil in a pan and gently toast half of the pittas for 2 minutes on each side until golden, turning over carefully. Remove to the baking tray and toast the remaining halves.

7. Bake for 8–12 minutes or until the pittas are crisp. Serve immediately with fresh vegetables.

Baked cauliflower sabich
With sumac onions

Sabich is yet another tasty Israeli street-food. Originally it was made by Jews of Iraqi decent, these are pittas loaded with fried aubergines (eggplants), hard-boiled eggs, pickles, salad, harissa, tahini and amba (unripe mango relish).

I came up with the idea to replace the aubergines with cauliflower from chef Bentzi Arbel when he started serving this twist on *sabich* at his eatery Mifgash Ha'osher a couple of years ago, Tel Avivians were lining up to try the new creation.

Here, I chose to bake the florets, but the fried ones on page 38 are equally delicious.

Whenever I order falafel or *shawarma*, I always add some sumac onions on top. Tangy, crisp and sharp, I think they are the ultimate accompaniment to any Middle Eastern pitta dish. It is an easy salad that is great to have in your repertoire. If you can't find good-quality ground sumac, you can replace it with curry powder to make a different salad, but one that's still good!

If you can't find pittas with a nice pocket, use sourdough bread and make sandwiches.

serves 3 / vegan / prep and cook: 40 minutes

Ingredients
For the cauliflower

1 small cauliflower
2–3 tablespoons olive oil
fine sea salt and freshly ground black pepper

For the sumac onion salad

1 medium-small sized onions, peeled and thinly sliced
1 scant teaspoon ground sumac
½ teaspoon sea salt
freshly squeezed lemon juice, to taste

To serve

3 regular or wholewheat pitta breads
homemade tahini sauce (see page 38)
3–4 pickled cucumbers, thinly sliced
1–2 tomatoes, thinly sliced
15 g (½ oz/small handful) parsley, finely chopped

Method

1. **To make the cauliflower:** Preheat the oven to 190°C (375°F/Gas 5) and line a baking tray (baking sheet) with parchment paper.

2. Steam the cauliflower whole (see page 24) for 7–8 minutes, or until just tender. Drain and transfer to a cutting board, then cut into medium-size florets. Roughly chop the stem of the cauliflower.

3. Place the florets and stem in a large bowl, add the oil and salt and pepper to taste, and toss gently to coat. Arrange them on the prepared baking tray and bake in the oven for 15–20 minutes until the florets are golden. Remove and allow to cool slightly.

4. **To make the salad:** While the cauliflower is steaming, place the onions, sumac and salt in a large bowl. Rub the salt onto the onions, then set aside for 20 minutes until the onions soften a little. Drain the onions, squeezing out any excess water then transfer to a clean bowl. Taste and hit it with more salt, or some fresh lemon juice if you like.

5. **To serve:** Remove the top of the pitta and fill with tahini, baked florets, onion salad and other toppings.

Colourful cauliflower popcorn
With Romanesco and oregano

Whenever you're on the lookout for cauliflower, keep your eyes (and mind) open for colourful caulis: green, purple, yellow and, of course, Romanesco, a vegetable so handsome most people forget to cook it.

Once you've had a chance to appreciate their beauty and invite them home, all you need is five minutes of work to turn them into a great starter or antipasti.

Unlike most recipes in the book for baked florets, here the cauliflowers are not steamed or precooked. When placed directly in the oven, the florets retain a nutty crunch. American food bloggers found the resulting texture to be reminiscent of popcorn, thus giving the dish its name and helping it go.

serves 5 / vegan / gluten-free / prep and cook: 45 minutes

Ingredients

1 medium or large cauliflower or 2 small colourful caulis
4–5 tablespoons olive oil
sea salt and freshly ground black pepper
½ teaspoon dried oregano

Method

1. Preheat the oven to 190°C (375°F/Gas 5) and line a baking tray (baking sheet) lined with parchment paper.

2. Cut the cauliflower into bite-size florets. Peel and roughly chop the main stem of the cauliflower.

3. Place the florets and stem in a large bowl, add the oil and salt and pepper to taste, and toss to coat. Lay them on the prepared baking tray .

4. Bake for 15 minutes. Carefully open the oven door and stir gently to turn the vegetables, then return them to the oven for a further 15–20 minutes until the florets are golden and just tender.

5. Remove and allow to cool slightly. Sprinkle over the oregano and serve warm or at room temperature.

6. Keeps refrigerated for up to four days.

Caulitip Any spice good enough for regular popcorn can be used instead of oregano. Try smoked paprika or za'atar.

Grandpa Lior's cauliflower
Braised in Spanish-style lemon, pepper and garlic sauce

During a Friday dinner with Adi's family, I asked her grandparents if they had any interesting cauliflower dishes up their sleeve. Her grandfather, Lior, paused for a moment, then told us that his mother used to make an excellent dish, one that he still enjoys preparing.

He told us that his mother learnt the dish from her neighbours in Neve Tzedek in Tel Aviv. They were of Spanish descent and had prepared the cauliflower in a unique way. First, it was cooked in water or steamed, then coated and fried, and finally braised in a lemony, slightly sweet pepper sauce.

This is alchemy in cooking at its best: taking a few quite humble ingredients and then creating something larger than the sum of their parts.

serves 3–4 / contains eggs / prep and cook: 1 hour

Ingredients

For the cauliflower

1 medium-size cauliflower
oil, for deep-frying
2–3 medium eggs, preferably free-range
125 g (4 oz/1 cup) plain (all-purpose) or wholewheat flour
½ teaspoon fine sea salt

For the sauce

2–3 tablespoons olive oil
2 red peppers, cored and diced into 2–3 cm (1 in) cubes
8 garlic cloves (or more), peeled and thinly sliced
1 red or green chilli, deseeded (you can use more or less to
 your liking) and thinly sliced
125 ml (4 fl oz/½ cup) freshly squeezed lemon juice
 (about 2–3 lemons)
about 750 ml (26 fl oz/3 cups) water
about 1 tablespoon demerara, muscovado or other brown sugar
sea salt and freshly ground black pepper

Method

1. **To cook the cauliflower:** Steam the cauliflower whole (see page 24) for 7–9 minutes, or until just tender. Transfer it to a large bowl and allow to cool slightly, then cut into medium-size florets.

2. Heat the oil for deep-frying in a small saucepan. Crack the eggs into a bowl and whisk well.

3. Mix the flour and salt in a bowl.

4. Coat the steamed florets with the flour, then dip in the egg batter until evenly coated.

5. Fry in 2–3 batches for 3–4 minutes or until nicely golden. Lift out with a slotted spoon and drain on kitchen paper (see picture opposite).

6. **To make the sauce:** Heat the oil in a medium-size pan. Add the peppers, garlic and chilli, and sweat over a medium heat for 4–5 minutes until just tender, while stirring frequently.

7. Add the lemon juice, fried florets and enough water to just cover the florets. Bring to the boil, season with salt, pepper and sugar, and simmer, uncovered, over a medium–low heat for 25 minutes, or until the florets are completely tender and the liquid has reduced by half (see picture overleaf).

8. Taste the sauce and adjust the seasoning with salt, pepper or sugar, if necessary. Serve warm or at room temperature.

9. The dish keeps refrigerated for up to 5 days.

Vegan: Coat the cauliflower in beer batter (see page 128) instead of the flour and egg coating.

Gluten-free: Use cornflour (cornstarch) or other gluten-free flours instead of the wheat flour.

Paleo: Omit the sugar and flour. Coat the cauliflower in superfine almond meal or just the egg.

Caulitip

To bake: Arrange the coated cauliflower on a baking tray (baking sheet) lined with parchment paper, drizzle each floret with olive oil and bake in a preheated oven at 200°C (400°F/Gas 6) for 15 minutes or until golden.

Cauliflower wings
A vegetarian version of a game-day classic

Aside from being two of the most viewed sports events in the world, the annual championship games of the NFL and MLB (known as the Superbowl and the World Series) are also major food events.

One iconic game day dish is buffalo wings – baked or fried until crispy and then covered with butter and hot sauce. A couple of years ago a vegetarian cauli-based version started circling about food blogs.

The recipe here is based on one published on the blog gimmedelicious.com, with some adjustments.

If three tablespoons of hot sauce are too much for you to handle, replace some or all of it with sweet chilli sauce. You can also play around with the spices; dried oregano, ground mustard seeds and coriander seeds all work well.

Note that the cauli-wings are crisp for only a short time, so this dish is best consumed immediately.

**serves 3 / vegan (omit the butter) /
prep and cook: 45 minutes**

Ingredients

1 medium-size cauliflower
140 g (4½ oz/heaped 1 cup) plain (all-purpose)
  or wholewheat flour
240 ml (6 fl oz/1 cup) water
1 teaspoon garlic powder
1 teaspoon sweet or smoked paprika
½ teaspoon ground cumin (optional)
3 tablespoons hot sauce of your liking (like sriracha
  or spicy chilli sauce)
2–3 tablespoons olive oil or melted butter
sea salt and freshly ground black pepper

Method

1. Preheat the oven to 200°C (400°F/Gas 6) and line a baking tray (baking sheet) with parchment paper.

2. Cut the cauliflower into bite-size florets.

3. In a bowl, whisk together the flour with most of the water until you have a batter the thickness of cream thick enough to coat a finger or spoon. Adjust with more water, if necessary. Add the garlic powder, paprika and cumin, if using, and season with salt and pepper.

4. Coat the florets in the batter and lay them on the prepared baking tray, leaving plenty of space between each floret.

5. Bake for 20–25 minutes until golden. Carefully remove from the oven.

6. In a large bowl, mix together the hot sauce and oil or butter. Add the baked florets and toss to coat.

7. Bake for a further 10–14 minutes until slightly charred.

8. Serve at once, with any other sauces and dips you fancy.

Caulitip

Gluten-free: Replace the flour with gluten-free flour, and make sure the sauces and spices you use are also gluten-free.

Shoflor: Moroccan-style cauliflower
With a garlic-tomato sauce

Yonit Tzukerman is quite a talented home cook and blogger who engages her followers each week by sharing her love for food over social media. She learned to cook from her Moroccan mother and grandmother, and this recipe is the one she was most excited to learn.

Here we have triple-cooked cauliflower, following the same steps as in grandpa Lior's cauliflower (see page 78). The delightful cuisines of Morocco and Spain share many common elements due to centuries of trade and conquest. The difference is in the sauce; based on fresh tomatoes and spice, which mingles with the florets to create a satisfying meaty sensation without any meat.

Nowadays Yonit prepares *shoflor* for her children. The name comes from the French word for cauliflower – the French ruled Morocco for over 40 years. Yonit says that just saying the name of the dish is enough to bring a smile to her children's faces.

serves 3–4 / contains eggs / prep and cook: 1 hour

Ingredients

For the cauliflower

1 medium-size cauliflower
oil, for deep-frying
2–3 medium eggs, preferably free-range
125 g (4 oz/1 cup) plain (all-purpose) or wholewheat flour
½ teaspoon sea salt
crusty bread, to serve

For the sauce

4–5 ripe tomatoes
2–3 tablespoons olive oil
5–6 garlic cloves, peeled, or more, thinly sliced
½ teaspoon ground turmeric
1 teaspoon hot or sweet paprika
500–750 ml (17–26 fl oz/2–3 cups) water
about 1 tablespoon demerara, muscovado
  or other brown sugar (to taste)
fine sea salt and freshly ground black pepper

Method

1. **To cook the cauliflower:** Steam the cauliflower whole (see page 24) for 7–9 minutes, or until just tender. Transfer to a large bowl and leave to cool slightly, then cut into medium-size florets.

2. Heat the oil for deep-frying in a small saucepan. Beat the eggs in a bowl. In another bowl, mix the flour and salt.

3. Coat the steamed florets with flour, then dip in the eggs until evenly coated.

4. Fry in 2–3 batches for 3–4 minutes, or until nicely golden (see picture opposite). Lift out with a slotted spoon and drain on kitchen paper.

5. **To make the sauce:** Grate the tomatoes and place in a bowl.

6. Heat the oil in a medium-size saucepan, add the garlic and cook, stirring frequently, over a medium heat for about until the garlic is fragrant but not brown.

7. Add the grated tomatoes, turmeric and paprika, and season with salt and pepper and stir well. Add the fried florets and enough water just to cover (see picture overleaf).

8. Bring to the boil, then simmer, uncovered, over a medium–low heat for 25 minutes, or until the florets are completely tender and the braising liquid has reduced by half.

9. Taste the sauce and adjust the seasoning if necessary with salt, black pepper or sugar. Serve warm or at room temperature – alongside some bread to mop up all the flavours.

10. The dish keeps refrigerated for 5 days.

Caulitip

Vegan: Coat the cauliflower in beer batter (see page 128) instead of the flour and egg coating.

Gluten-free: Use cornflour (cornstarch) or other gluten-free flours instead of the wheat flour

Paleo: Omit the sugar and flour. Coat the cauliflower in superfine almond meal or only with egg.

To bake: Arrange the coated florets on a baking tray (baking sheet) with parchment paper, drizzle with a little oil and bake at 200°C (400°F/Gas 6) for 15 minutes until golden.

Patties and fritters

Raheli's cauliflower–corn nuggets
Baked or fried

Raheli Krut (see page 239, bottom picture, with sunglasses) is the editor of this book's Hebrew edition and a true wonder woman: a writer, designer, stylist, blogger and, above all, a real friend.

She has stood by me from the beginning of my career as a food writer, and was my first real editor. I called her 'my chef Ramsay' because whenever I sent her a piece of writing or a recipe that wasn't good enough, she made it very clear (in a nice way!). With her guidance, I learnt how important it is to listen to your readers, to pay attention to every tiny detail and remember you are always rewarded for hard, honest work.

These crunchy nuggets are one of her favourite recipes: fun to make and shape, easy to prepare ahead and oh-so irresistible. They can serve as a light vegetarian dinner or a lovely snack for young and old alike, and are as good baked as they are fried.

makes 30–40 nuggets / contains dairy and eggs / prep and cook: 1½ hours

Ingredients

1 small-medium cauliflower
1 large potato, cooked and peeled
2 medium eggs, preferably free-range
125 g (4 oz) Gouda or Cheddar cheese, grated
kernels from 2 corn cobs
  or 150 g (5 oz/¾ cup) frozen
corn kernels (no need to defrost)
½ teaspoon sea salt
100 g (3½ oz/¾ cup) plain (all-purpose) flour

To coat and fry or bake

60 g (2 oz/1 cup) breadcrumbs (preferably panko)
2 tablespoons sesame seeds
750 ml (25 fl oz/3 cups) oil, for deep-frying,
  or 3–4 tablespoons oil, for baking

Method

1. If you are baking, preheat the oven to 190°C (375°F/ Gas 5) and line a baking tray (baking sheet) with baking parchment.

2. Steam the cauliflower whole (see page 24) for 11–13 minutes until tender but not completely soft. Cut into florets and reserve the stem and stalks for other uses. Alternatively, put in a bowl and microwave the florets with 120 ml (4 fl oz/½ cup) of water for 8 minutes until just tender.

3. In a large bowl, mash the cooked potato, add the florets and continue mashing until the cauliflower is broken into small bits but still retains some texture.

4. Crack in the eggs and add the cheese, corn kernels and salt. Mix well, then stir in the flour to create a thick, slightly sticky mass (see picture opposite). Cover with cling film (plastic wrap) and chill for 30 minutes.

5. Using wet hands to stop the mixture sticking to you, shape a heaped tablespoon of the mixture into a ball or nugget and put on the prepared baking tray. Repeat with the rest of the mixture (see picture overleaf).

6. In a shallow bowl, mix the breadcrumbs with the sesame seeds. Coat the nuggets in the mixture, then return them to the baking tray (see picture overleaf).

7. **If baking:** Drizzle the nuggets with the oil. The more oil you use, the crispier they will be. Bake for 12–15 minutes until golden.

8. **If frying:** Heat the oil for deep-frying in a small/medium, heavy-based pan. Fry 4–5 nuggets at a time for 3–5 minutes until golden. Lift out with a slotted spoon and drain on paper towels (see picture overleaf).

9. Serve at once, with any dip you like and a side salad. The nuggets keep well in the fridge for four days and can be frozen for up to three months.

Caulitip

Gluten-Free: Replace the plain flour with chickpea or red lentil flour. Use gluten-free or cornflakes crumbs.

Vegan: Replace the cheese and eggs with 120 g (4 oz/scant ⅔ cup) of mashed silken tofu mixed with 2 tablespoons of chickpea or red lentil flour and 1 teaspoon of miso paste. Add a little water if the mixture is too thick.

A'rouk
Iraqi-style herb and potato patties with chopped fresh cauliflower

A'rouk is an Iraqi dish of patties made from eggs, mashed potatoes and fresh herbs. Jews of Iraqi descent, like my grandmother, Hanna, and her family, usually serve a'rouk with fried aubergine (eggplants) and a chopped lemon salad as a light lunch every Friday before the heavier Shabbat dinner.

I love these patties in any state: hot from the pan, lukewarm and even cold, in sandwiches and pittas with sliced tomatoes and tahini sauce (see page 38). When you have any kind of fresh herbs left over, you can make a'rouk.

Cauliflower is not included in a'rouk – Iraqis mainly pickle it (see page 53). However, I added some freshly chopped cauliflower to my grandma's recipe, and the experiment was a great success.

During its time in the pan, the cauliflower gets just a little bit tender, retaining a mellow crunch that upgrades this already great patty.

serves 4 (makes about 20 patties) / contains eggs / prep and cook: 1 hour

Ingredients

2–3 medium-size potatoes, scrubbed
¼ small cauliflower or 3–4 medium-size florets
2–3 spring onions (scallions), cut into tiny rings
about 75 g (2½ oz/small bunch) parsley, finely chopped
½ teaspoon ground cumin, or more to taste
1 scant teaspoon paprika (sweet or hot)
1 teaspoon sea salt
2 tablespoons plain (all-purpose) or wholewheat flour
1–2 large eggs, preferably free-range
olive oil, for shallow frying
tahini sauce (see page 38), sliced tomatoes and Turshi
  (see page 53) (optional)

Method

1. Cook the potatoes in their skins in a small pan of boiling water for 30–40 minutes until soft. Alternatively, cook them in a covered microwave-safe bowl with 120 ml (4 fl oz, ½ cup) of water for 12–15 minutes until soft.

2. Carefully remove the skins from the hot potatoes, then transfer them to a large bowl. Mash with a fork, then leave to cool slightly.

3. Cut the cauliflower into florets and finely chop them using a knife to give you that uneven texture.

4. Add the spring onions, parsley, cumin, paprika, salt and flour to the potatoes and mix well to combine.

5. Crack in one egg and mix again. If the mixture feels dry, add the second egg and mix to combine.

6. Gently stir in the cauliflower (see picture opposite). If you have time, cover the bowl with cling film (plastic wrap) and refrigerate for 20–30 minutes.

7. Heat the oil in a wide non-stick pan over a medium-high heat. Using wet hands to stop the mixture sticking to you, take about a heaped tablespoon of the mixture and shape into a 1 cm (½ in) thick round patty shape.

8. Lay 5–6 patties in the pan and fry for 3–4 minutes on one side, then 1–2 minutes on the other until golden on both sides (see picture overleaf). Use a spatula to transfer to a plate lined with kitchen paper, then shape and fry the patties from the remaining mixture.

9. Serve with tahini, tomatoes and some turshi, if you like.

Caulitip

Gluten-free: Replace the wheat flour with chickpea or red lentil flour.

Vegan: Replace the eggs with 2 heaped tablespoons of chickpea or red lentil flour mixed with 4 tablespoons of water.

Paleo: Omit the flour completely (the mixture will be a bit wet, but still workable).

To bake: Lay the shaped patties on a baking tray (baking sheet) lined with parchment paper. Brush with olive oil and bake in a preheated oven at 200°C (400°F/ Gas 6) for 10 minutes until golden.

Cauliflower and cheese patties
Five-ingredient magic

When I started thinking about which recipes should make it into the book, these patties were on the top of the list. I first published them a couple of years ago on my blog. They are especially popular during the time of Hanukah – the Jewish holiday which allows you to fry and deep-fry with no remorse. Yay!

The mix of cauliflower and cheese is well celebrated throughout the world (the Scottish even add whisky to their cauli-cheese bakes), and the aroma of golden cauliflower along with the beautiful richness of the cheese is nothing short of heavenly.

The preparation is very straightforward with few ingredients, and I hope these patties will become one of your household staples.

If you prefer baking rather than frying, lay the formed patties on a baking tray (baking sheet) lined with parchment paper. Brush with olive oil and bake in a pre-heated oven at 200° (400°F/ Gas 6) for 10–12 minutes until golden.

serves 3–4 (makes 10–12 patties) / contains dairy and eggs / prep and cook: 30 minutes

Ingredients
1 small cauliflower
2 medium eggs, preferably free-range
100 g (3½ oz) Mozzarella, Gouda or Cheddar cheese, grated
1 spring onion (scallion), green and white parts thinly sliced
3–4 tablespoons breadcrumbs or oatmeal
sea salt
olive oil, for shallow-frying

Method
1. Cut the cauliflower into medium-size florets. Place in a microwave-safe bowl with 120 ml (4 fl oz/½ cup) of water, cover and microwave for 8 minutes until tender. Or, you can boil or steam the florets (see page 24).

2. Drain off the water, then mash using a fork.

3. Add the eggs, cheese, spring onion, breadcrumbs or oatmeal and salt, then stir to combine.

4. Heat the oil in a wide non-stick pan over a medium-high heat. Using wet hands to stop the mixture sticking to you, take about a heaped tablespoon from the mixture and shape into a 1 cm (½ in) thick round patty shape.

5. Lay 5–6 patties in the pan and fry for 2–3 minutes on each side until nice and golden.

6. Use a slotted spoon to transfer to a plate lined with kitchen paper, then continue shaping and frying patties from the remaining mixture. Serve immediately.

Cauli tip

Gluten-Free: Replace the wheat flour with chickpea or red lentil flour.

Vegan: Replace the cheese and eggs with 120 g (4 oz) mashed silken tofu mixed with 2 tablespoons of chickpea or red lentil flour and 1 teaspoon of miso paste, adding a little water if the mixture is too thick.

Cauli-burger
An Instagram hit

On a cold and rainy day, Raheli Krut, editor of this book's Hebrew edition, was craving a juicy burger. When she opened up her fridge and freezer she found no meat; all she had was a head of cauliflower and a bunch of herbs, so she dreamed up this brilliant herbaceous burger recipe.

When she posted a photo of the burger Instagram (you can follow her @raheli), she was totally overwhelmed with responses and recipe requests, and I knew that I wanted to include her idea in this book.

These vegetarian burgers go really well inside a bun or a pitta, served with some yoghurt, fries, sour cream, lettuce, tomato and other trimmings.

The mixture should feel slightly soft yet hold its shape, so add extra some breadcrumbs if it feels too loose. And feel free to play around with different herbs, chopped spring onions (scallions) or fresh oregano, even a chopped chilli makes a great addition if you a bit of heat.

See the recipe for A'rouk on page 94 for an easy vegan egg alternative.

**makes 8–10 burgers / contains eggs /
prep and cook: 1 hour**

Ingredients

1 medium-size cauliflower
10–15 basil leaves
about 30 g (1 oz) chives
about 60 g (2 oz) parsley or coriander (cilantro)
3 medium eggs, preferably free-range
50 g (2 oz/¾ cup) breadcrumbs
4 tablespoons red lentil or chickpea flour
40 g (1½ oz/⅓ cup) oatmeal (optional)
sea salt and coarsely ground black pepper
2–4 tablespoons olive oil, for brushing
burger buns, lettuce, tomatoes, yoghurt and mayonnaise,
  to serve

Method

1. Steam the cauliflower whole (see page 24) for 11–13 minutes until tender but not completely soft. Allow to drain and cool to room temperature. Cut into florets and transfer to a bowl.

2. Mash the florets using a fork or potato masher – you want a rough mash with little flowers visible.

3. Finely chop all the herbs and add to the cauliflower, with all the remaining ingredients and mix to combine. Cover with cling film (plastic wrap) and refrigerate for 30 minutes.

4. Preheat the oven to 180°C (350°F/Gas 4), line a baking tray (baking sheet) with parchment paper and brush with oil.

5. Using wet hands to stop the mixture sticking to you, divide the mixture to 8–10 equal-size balls, place them on the lined baking tray and gently press to burger shapes about 1 cm (½ inch) thick. Brush or drizzle the patties with oil.

6. Bake for 15–20 minutes or until golden, flipping the burgers halfway through. Alternatively, shallow–fry the burgers for 2–4 minutes on each side until golden (flipping carefully with a metal spatula as the mixture is quite delicate).

7. Serve between burger buns with lettuce, tomatoes and yoghurt or mayonnaise.

Cauliflower and red lentil falafel
Fried along with friends

Falafel is considered by many to be one of Israel's national dishes, popular not only in street food stands but also in local restaurants and bars. I find the aroma of these crunchy, herby spiced balls irresistible, especially in the brief moments after they are lifted from the hot frying oil.

Originally from Egypt (or Yemen, depending on who you ask), falafel is most often made with soaked broad (fava) beans or chickpeas ground together with spices and herbs then deep-fried until super-crisp balls. Cauliflower is a good friend of typical falafel ingredients, adding a nutty note and surprising texture to these crunchy delicacies.

Here I use red lentils in place of the beans: they are similar in nutritional value, they require much less soaking time and yield an excellent crunch. You can also make a classic hummus from these lentils, but that's a whole other book.

When making falafel at home, remember it is like serving a soufflé: the guests wait for the falafel, not the other way around!

**serves 4–5 / vegan / gluten-free /
prep and cook: 3 hours**

Ingredients
400 g (14 oz/2 cups) red or orange lentils, well rinsed
about 75 g (2½ oz) parsley and/or coriander (cilantro)
⅓ small cauliflower or 3–4 florets
1 scant teaspoon ground cumin and/or ground coriander
sea salt and coarse black pepper, to taste
1–3 tablespoons red lentil or chickpea (gram) flour, if needed
vegetable oil, for deep-frying
tahini sauce (see page 38), salad and pittas, to serve

Method
1. Place the lentils in a bowl, cover with plenty of water and soak for 2 hours.

2. Coarsely chop the herbs and cauliflower.

3. Strain the lentils and leave them to drain well. Transfer to the bowl of a food processor with the herbs and cauliflower and pulse until you have a rough yet uniform mixture.

4. Transfer to a large bowl, add the spices and season with salt and pepper. Knead the mixture with your hands until well blended.

5. Heat the oil for deep-frying in a medium, deep saucepan.

6. To test your mixture, take a tablespoonful of the mixture with your hand and tighten into a ball. If the ball crumbles and feels wet, gradually work in some red lentil or chickpea flour until the mixture binds together.

7. Using wet hands to stop the mixture from sticking to you, shape little falafel balls and fry in small batches in the hot oil for 3–5 minutes, until golden-brown and crisp.

8. Serve at once, with tahini, salad and pittas.

Caulitip
To bake: Lay the shaped falafel balls on a baking tray lined with parchment paper. Drizzle very generously with olive oil and bake in a preheated oven at 200°C (400°F/Gas 6) for 12 minutes until golden brown.

Soups

Cauliflower–coconut crown soup
Garnished with smoky baby florets

This regal soup matches the delicate, nutty cauliflower with smoked paprika, which is a pumped up version of sweet paprika made by drying and smoking fresh sweet (or hot) chillies. It is an all-time favourite of mine.

When I serve this soup at home, I like arranging a circle of tiny florets on top. My wife (who is, of course, my queen) says it looks like a crown.

You can use coconut cream or milk here. I prefer cream. Make sure you choose one that has at least 18 per cent fat, and be sure it contains only coconut solids and water. Brands that contain unnecessary emulsifiers, stabilisers and preservatives should be avoided.

By all means, use more cream if you like. If you have leftover coconut cream, just freeze it in small containers for up to three months – it will be great for cooking.

If preferred, you can always use double (heavy) cream instead of coconut cream.

serves 3–4 / vegan / prep and cook: 40 minutes

Ingredients

For the soup

1 large cauliflower
750 ml–1 litre (25–34 fl oz/3–4 cups) water
80 ml (3 fl oz/⅓ cup) coconut cream, or more if you like
sea salt

For the garnish

3–4 tablespoons coconut or olive oil
½ teaspoon smoked paprika
sea salt
½ teaspoon dried chilli flakes (optional)
1 tablespoon fried shallots (optional)

Method

1. **To make the soup:** Cut the cauliflower into even-size florets, set 4 florets aside for the garnish. Peel and roughly chop the stem (reserve the stalks for making stock).

2. Place the florets and stem in a medium-size saucepan and just cover with water. Bring to the boil over a high heat, then cook, uncovered, over a medium heat for 14–18 minutes or until the florets are completely tender and easily mashed with a fork.

3. Remove about half of the cooking liquid from the pan and set aside. Add the coconut cream and purée using a hand-held blender for 2–3 minutes, or until you reach a very smooth, cream-like consistency, add more cooking liquid, if necessary. Season with salt to taste.

4. **To make the garnish:** Cut the reserved florets into baby flowers about size of a peanut. Place in a frying pan along with the oil and sauté over a high heat, stirring frequently for 4–5 minutes, until the florets are tender and golden.

5. Add the paprika and season with salt. The florets should take on a lovely red-orange colour.

6. To serve, divide the soup between serving bowls, garnish with the baby florets and their red oil and sprinkle with chilli flakes and fried shallots if you like.

Seared cauliflower and miso soup
With crispy tofu

Miso is an umami-rich soy bean paste, created in China and now popular in Japan. Today you can find it in almost every market. The deep, complex flavour goes really well with the buttery notes of cauliflower in this creamy soup.

To get the cauliflower golden without using a lot of oil, I halved it lengthways. That way the florets have more contact area with the pan and they get golden quite quickly. Pre-searing can give a serious flavour boost to any cauliflower cream or mash you make. If you want the golden cauliflower flavour but are not in the mood for searing, go ahead and bake your florets (see page 29).

For another Japanese touch, drizzle two or three drops of toasted sesame oil into each serving bowl.

serves 3–4 / vegan / prep and cook: 40 minutes

Ingredients

For the soup
1 large cauliflower
3–4 tablespoons olive oil or vegetable oil
750 ml–1 litre (25–34 fl oz/3–4 cups) water
1 heaped tablespoon light or dark miso paste
sea salt

For the garnish
3–4 tablespoons olive oil or vegetable oil
185 g (6½ oz/1 cup) firm tofu, cut into 1 cm (½ in) cubes
1–2 spring onions (scallions), cut into rings
2–3 teaspoons black or toasted sesame seeds

Method

1. **To make the soup:** Cut the cauliflower into large florets. Halve the florets lengthways.

2. Heat the oil in a wide pan. Place one layer of florets cut-side down and sear for 2–3 minutes, or until golden (on one side only). Transfer to a medium-size saucepan and repeat with the remaining florets.

3. Cover with water and bring to the boil over a high heat. Cook, uncovered, over a medium heat for 16–18 minutes, or until the florets are completely tender. Remove about half of the cooking liquid from the pan and set aside.

4. In a small bowl, stir the miso paste with 120 ml (4 fl oz/ ½ cup) of the reserved cooking liquid until dissolved, then add to the pan.

5. Using a hand-held blender, purée the soup for 2–3 minutes or until you reach a very smooth, cream-like consistency, add more cooking liquid, if necessary. Season with salt to taste (but remember the miso is quite salty on its own).

6. **To make the garnish:** Heat the oil in a small frying pan. Add the tofu and fry over a medium-high heat, stirring occasionally, for about 3 minutes until golden and crisp.

7. To serve, divide the soup between bowls and garnish with the tofu, spring onion and sesame seeds.

Grandma's cauliflower-dill soup
Winter comfort!

Every time my sisters and I visit our grandmother during winter, we hope this soup will be there. One taste of this steaming bowl is all it takes to transport me back to my childhood – we used to fight over the large chunks of cauliflower, so tender you could cut through them with your serving spoon.

Grandma Hanna says she picked up the recipe from an old cookbook a few decades ago, and it quickly became a family favourite. Even those who don't normally like dill enjoy this soup! I added one small addition to Grandma's recipe: black lentils, which give the soup a dark colour and deep flavour.

Serves 4–5 / vegan / prep and cook: 1 hour

Ingredients

1 large cauliflower
3–4 tablespoons olive oil or vegetable oil
1 tablespoon plain (all-purpose) flour
150 g (5 oz/¾ cup) black, Puy or green lentils, well rinsed
  about 60 g (2 oz, small bunch) fresh dill, roughly chopped
1¼–1½ litres (44–53 fl oz/5–6 cups) water
sea salt

Method

1. Cut the cauliflower into florets, peel and roughly chop the main stem and roughly chop the stalks and leaves.

2. Heat the oil in a medium-size saucepan. Add all the parts of the cauliflower and cook over a medium-high heat for 10 minutes until slightly tender, stirring occasionally.

3. Add the flour and stir well. Add most of the dill, the lentils and enough water to come up to 4 cm (1½ in) above the cauliflower. Stir well and bring to the boil, then season generously with salt.

4. Cover and simmer over a low heat for 25–35 minutes until all parts of the cauliflower are completely tender and the lentils are soft but not mushy.

5. Stir in the remaining dill, taste and adjust with more salt if needed and serve.

6. The soup keeps well in the fridge for 3–4 days.

Caulitip

Gluten-free: Omit the flour and add an extra 50 g (2 oz/¼ cup) of lentils.

You can replace the dill with other fresh herbs such as parsley or coriander (cilantro).

For a more intense flavour, add 2–3 tablespoons of light soy sauce along with the lentils.

Cauliflower and beetroot borscht
A tangy Soviet classic

Borscht is a classic Eastern European soup, prepared in countless ways with a vast variety of ingredients from potatoes and beans to beef, pork and even porcini mushrooms. Aside from the beetroot (beet) and vinegar, which are the most iconic borscht ingredients, many Ukrainian and Russian recipes have cabbage (and even sauerkraut).

Here, I replace the cabbage with cauliflower, which takes on a light crimson colour from the powerful betaine pigments in the beetroot.

If you prefer your soup creamy rather than chunky, use a hand-held blender to purée the soup once it's cooked (just don't forget to pick out the bay leaves first). For a smooth and creamy texture, add a few tablespoons of olive oil while puréeing the soup.

serves 4–5 / vegan (omit sour cream) / prep and cook: 1 hour

Ingredients

For the soup

1 large cauliflower
3–4 tablespoons olive oil or vegetable oil
1 large onion, diced into medium-size cubes
1 heaped tablespoon tomato purée (paste)
4 medium-size beetroots (beets), peeled and diced
  into medium-size cubes
2 bay leaves
3–4 tablespoons apple cider vinegar or red wine vinegar
980 ml–1½ litres (37–44 fl oz/4–5 cups) water
1 teaspoon fine sea salt, plus more to taste
1 teaspoon brown sugar (optional)

To serve

150 ml (5 fl oz/⅔ cup) full-fat sour cream or crème fraîche
a small handful of fresh dill fronds (optional)
coarsely ground black pepper

Method

1. Cut the cauliflower into medium-size florets, peel and roughly chop the main stem and roughly chop the stalks and leaves.

2. Heat the oil in a medium-size saucepan. Add the onion and chopped cauliflower stem, stalks and leaves, and fry over a medium-low heat for about 8 minutes, stirring occasionally until slightly tender.

3. Add the tomato paste (purée) and cook, stirring, for one minute. Add the beetroot, florets, bay leaves, vinegar and enough water to come up to about 4 cm (1½ in) above the contents of the saucepan.

4. Bring the soup to the boil, cover, then simmer over a medium-low heat for 30 minutes, until the vegetables are tender. Taste and season with salt and more vinegar, if you like; add sugar if the acidity needs balancing.

5. To serve, divide the soup among bowls and add a dollop of cream to each. Sprinkle the dill and some black pepper on top. Keeps refrigerated for 3–4 days.

Winter vegetable garden soup
With Hungarian nokedli

This recipe is from the book's photographer, Assaf Ambram. For generations, members of the Hungarian side of Assaf's family have been preparing this humble yet gratifying soup on rainy days. According to Assaf, this vegetable-packed soup is especially loved by the young ones in the family.

This soup traditionally includes *nokedli*, which are delicate, chewy-yet-fluffy quick-cooking dumplings, that are very similar to *spätzle*. If you happen to have a spätzli maker, use it to make the *nokedli*. You can buy one online or in most kitchen stores.

You can, of course, omit the *nokedli* and serve the soup with homemade croûtons. Alternatively, replace the *nokedli* with store-bought potato gnocchi, cooked according to the instructions on the packet, and added to the hot soup.

serves 4 / contains meat and/or eggs / prep and cook: 1 hour

Ingredients

For the soup

1 medium cauliflower
2 tablespoons olive oil
1 large onion, peeled and diced into medium-size cubes
2–3 large carrots, peeled and cut into matchsticks
1 large parsnip, peeled and cut into matchsticks
1 tablespoon plain (all-purpose) flour
980 ml–1¼ litres (34–44 fl oz/4–5 cups) chicken, cauliflower
  or vegetable stock or water
130 g (4 oz/1 cup) frozen peas (no need to defrost)
about 60 g (2 oz/small bunch of) parsley, roughly chopped
sea salt and freshly ground black pepper, to taste

For the nokedli (dumplings)

3 large eggs, preferably free-range
140 g (4¾ oz/heaped 1 cup) plain (all-purpose) flour
½ teaspoon sea salt to season the nokedli,
  plus 1 tablespoon to season the cooking water
1–2 tablespoons water (if needed)

Method

1. **For the soup:** Cut the cauliflower into small florets, peel the main stem, cut it into matchsticks and finely chop the stalks and leaves.

2. Heat the oil in a medium-size saucepan. Add the onion, carrots, parsnip and cauliflower (all parts), sweat over a medium heat for 10 minutes, stirring occasionally, until the onion softens and is translucent (see picture opposite).

3. Add the flour and stir well. Add the stock or water (it should come up to about 4 cm (1½ in) above the content of the saucepan) along with the peas, and bring to the boil over a high heat, while stirring.

4. Season with salt and pepper, then add half of the parsley and stir well.

5. Simmer over low heat for 45 minutes, until the vegetables are soft and the soup has slightly thickened.

6. **To make the nokedli**: Crack the eggs into a bowl and add the flour and salt. Stir well, using a fork, until you have a thick pancake-like batter. If the mixture is too thick (not runny at all), gradually add a little water to loosen it.

7. Bring a medium-size saucepan of water to the boil. Add 1 tablespoon of salt. Take a small teaspoonful of the nokedli mixture, hold the spoon above the boiling water and allow it to drop to the water, creating tiny dumplings (see picture overleaf). Continue with the rest of the mixture. Cook the dumplings for 5 minutes until set and chewy, then strain and stir into the hot soup.

8. Stir the remaining parsley into the soup. Taste and adjust the seasoning, if necessary.

9. Serve with croutons, only if you didn't make the nokedli.

Gluten-free: Omit the flour and nokedli. Add 2 finely diced potatoes to the soup along with the peas.

Upgrade your nokedli mix by adding 1–2 tablespoons of snipped chives, coarse black pepper or ¼ teaspoon freshly grated nutmeg.

Caulitip

Feel free to add more veggies to the soup: chopped leek or matchsticks from a small celeriac (celery root) or kohlrabi would make great additions.

If you want a thicker soup, use a hand-held blender to purée just enough to thicken the soup (before adding the nokedli).

Far Eastern cauliflower

Easy aloo gobi
With a Yemenite twist

Aloo gobi (which means potato and cauliflower) is a stewed vegetable dish typical in northern India.

Traditional recipes for this dish included a long list of spices. Admittedly, I have yet to posses the deep insights and spice wisdom of Indian cooks, but there is one spice mix I love to use at home that fits right in here. It is called *hawaij*, and it is the signature spice blend of Yemen.

*Hawaij*g consists of ground turmeric, fenugreek, cloves, coriander, cumin, cardamom (and more, depending on the blend), and adds colour and depth to many hearty chicken or meat soups. Many Jews of Yemenite descent use it in their daily cooking. I like adding it to lentil soups and fish stews.

Here *hawaij* forms a base flavour for the dish, greatly shortening the ingredients list. You can find it in spice shops or you can order it online. If it you can't get a hold if it, good-quality curry powder also works.

serves 3–4 / vegan / prep and cook: 40 minutes

Ingredients
1 medium-size cauliflower
3 tablespoons olive oil
1 teaspoon whole cumin seeds (optional)
1 medium-size onion, peeled and diced into medium-size cubes
4–6 garlic cloves, peeled and thinly sliced
3 medium (unpeeled) potatoes, diced to 2½ cm (1 in) cubes
1 scant tablespoons hawaij or good-quality curry powder
350 ml (12 fl oz/1½ cups) water
2 tablespoons freshly squeezed lemon juice (optional)
sea salt and freshly ground black pepper
a handful of fresh coriander (cilantro) leaves, to garnish
steamed rice and Spicy Green Herb Salsa
  (see page 58), to serve

Method
1. Cut the cauliflower into small florets. Thinly slice the stalks and leaves, peel and roughly chop the main stem.

2. Heat the oil in a medium-size saucepan. Add the cumin seeds, onion, garlic, cauliflower stalks and stem, and sauté over a high heat for 3–4 minutes until the onion softens and appears translucent, stirring frequently.

3. Add the potatoes and florets and sauté for a further 2 minutes, then add the hawaij and stir.

4. Add the water, season with salt and pepper. Stir well – the water will not cover the content of the pan and that's fine (we are cooking using steam here). Bring to the boil, cover the pan and cook over a medium heat for 18–24 minutes until the potatoes and florets are completely tender. Stir every once in a while, and if the bottom of the pan appears too dry, add a little more water.

5. Once tender, remove the lid and continue cooking until almost all the water has evaporated. Add the lemon juice, if using, and stir gently.

6. Divide among serving plates, garnish with coriander leaves and serve with steamed rice and green salsa.

7. This will keep refrigerated for 4 days.

Green vegetable curry
With greens and cauliflower

In a small restaurant in the city of Kanchanaburi in Thailand, I had an absolutely wonderful green curry dish. It was prepared by a chef named On. On also gives cooking lessons for those visiting the city, known worldwide for the bridge on the River Kwai. Inspired by her dish, I share this recipe with you.

My green curry paste is not a traditional one. Thai chefs claim that in order for a paste to be authentic, it must be ground and pounded by hand with a mortar and pestle for 30–40 minutes. Given our limited time to cook, using a food processor is a helpful short cut.

You can, of course, use store-bought curry paste – just add some freshly chopped coriander (cilantro) stems to your dish.

This and other Thai-inspired dishes in the book call for an important south-east Asian ingredient – fish sauce or *nam pla*. Made by salting and fermenting anchovies, it adds a unique umami kick. You can find it today in most supermarkets or Asian grocery stores.

serves 3 / contains fish / prep and cook: 45 minutes

Ingredients

For the green curry paste

2–3 green chillies
about 60 g (2 oz/½ bunch) coriander (cilantro)
2½ cm (1 in) piece of fresh root ginger, peeled
1 small red onion or 4–5 shallots, peeled
2 lemongrass stalks (optional)
5–6 garlic cloves, peeled
1 teaspoon sea salt

For the vegetables

1 small cauliflower
150 g (5 oz) mangetout (snow peas) or green beans, trimmed
1 medium-size courgette (zucchini), diced into 1 cm (½ in) cubes
100 g (3½ oz, a large handful) frozen peas

For the curry

1 tablespoon olive or coconut oil
2–4 tablespoons green curry paste (see above)
240 ml (8 fl oz/1 cup) high-fat coconut cream
120 ml (4 fl oz/½ cup) water
2 dried or fresh kaffir lime leaves (optional)
1 tablespoon Thai fish sauce
1 teaspoon palm or brown sugar
sea salt, to taste
boiled rice (see page 142), to serve

Method

1. **To make the curry paste:** Deseed the chillies if you prefer a milder flavour. Separate the coriander leaves and stems, reserving the leaves for garnish. Roughly chop all the paste ingredients.

2. Place all the paste ingredients into food processor and blitz to form a smooth paste (see pictures overleaf).

3. **To prepare the vegetables:** Cut the cauliflower into bite-size florets.

4. **To make the curry:** Heat the oil in a medium-size saucepan. Add the curry paste and fry over a medium-high heat for 30 seconds, or until fragrant. Gradually add the coconut cream, 3–4 tablespoons at a time. Stir well to combine. Add the water and bring to the boil. Add the kaffir lime leaves and fish sauce.

5. Add all the vegetables to the pan, then add a little more water or coconut cream to just cover the vegetables.

6. Bring to a strong boil and cook over a high heat for 2 minutes, until the vegetables are just tender yet firm to the bite.

7. Taste and add the fish sauce and sugar (or salt) to your liking.

8. Transfer to serving dishes, garnish with coriander (cilantro) leaves and serve with rice. The remaining paste can be refrigerated for one week or frozen for up to 6 months.

Vegan: Replace the fish sauce with light soy sauce or salt.

Any fast-cooking green veggie can join this curry. Try asparagus, broccoli or Thai aubergine (eggplant).

Cauli**tip**

The picture shows the fresh greens stand at the Kanchanaburi market.

Cauliflower pakora
With minted poppy seed yoghurt

Pakora means 'something small' in Hindi and, when applied to food, it usually describes fried vegetables in chickpea (gram) flour batter, most famous of which is the onion pakora, also referred to as onion bhaji.

Chickpea flour is quite a versatile ingredient, and is very popular within Indian cuisine. When mixed with water, it forms a gluten-free batter that, when fried, gets super crisp.

Pakora recipes typically call for various spices. Here I worked only with the bare essentials. Feel free to add a teaspoon of a spice or blend (say hot paprika or garam masala).

serves 2–3 / contains dairy / gluten-free / prep and cook: 20 minutes

Ingredients

For the cauliflower

oil, for deep-frying
1 medium-small cauliflower
125 g (4 oz/1 cup) chickpea (gram) or red lentil flour
½ teaspoon sea salt
180 ml (6½ fl oz/¾ cup) water

For the yoghurt

leaves from 4–5 mint sprigs
180 g (6½ oz/¾ cup) natural yoghurt (3% fat or more)
1 teaspoon poppy seeds
2–3 teaspoons freshly squeezed lemon juice
fine sea salt and freshly ground black pepper

Method

1. Heat the oil in a small saucepan.

2. Cut the cauliflower to bite-size florets.

3. In a large bowl, whisk the chickpea (gram) flour and salt with 120 ml (4 fl oz/½ cup) of water to form a batter the consistency of double (heavy) cream. If it is too thick, gradually add the remaining water. When you dip a spoon in the batter it should coat it, but not heavily.

4. When the oil is hot, coat the florets in the batter.

5. Fry in small batches for 4–5 minutes or until nicely golden and crisp. Lift out with a slotted spoon and drain on kitchen paper.

6. **To prepare the yoghurt:** Finely chop the mint leaves and place in small bowl. Stir in the yoghurt and poppy seeds. Taste and season with lemon juice and salt to taste. Serve with the pakoras.

Vegan: Omit the yoghurt and serve pakoras with homemade tahini sauce (see page 38) or on top of hummus.

Cauli**tip**

General Tso's cauliflower
Stir fried in ginger, garlic sweet-and-sour soy sauce

Almost every Western Chinese restaurant you'll come across will feature general Tso's chicken. First coated and fried, then tossed in a sweet and sour sauce, this popular dish gives Colonel Sanders a run for his money.

Cauliflower can easily stand in as a vegetarian substitute for the chicken in this dish, as many food bloggers have shown (I found the version made by bakeaholicmama.com to be most captivating).

This and other recipes in the book call for dark soy sauce. This thick and deep sauce is nothing more than regular soy sauce combined with dark molasses. Add just the right amount and you are a winner; add too much and you're in trouble. If you don't have dark soy sauce in your pantry just add a bit more light soy sauce and brown sugar.

serves 2–3 / vegan / prep and cook: 30 minutes

Ingredients

For the beer battered cauliflower

1 small cauliflower
2 heaped tablespoons self-raising (self-rising) flour
2 heaped tablespoons cornflour (cornstarch)
1/4 teaspoon fine salt
240 ml (8 fl oz/1 cup) cold light beer or soda water

For the sauce

3–4 garlic cloves, peeled
2 cm (¾ in) piece of fresh root ginger, peeled
2 spring onions (scallions), both green and white parts
1–3 small dried chillies or fresh red chillies
1–2 tablespoons oil, plus extra for deep-frying
about 2–3 tablespoons water
2 tablespoons light soy sauce
1 teaspoon dark soy sauce
1/2 tablespoon vinegar, such as apple cider or rice wine vinegar
1 tablespoon brown sugar (whatever kind you have)

Method

1. Thinly slice the garlic, finely chop the ginger and chop the spring onions to about 5 cm (2 in) in length. Using scissors, snip the dried chillies to small rings (or thinly slice the fresh red chillies).

2. **To cook the cauliflower:** Steam the cauliflower whole (see page 24) for 7–9 minutes until the florets are just tender. Remove from the saucepan and let the cauliflower cool down a bit. Cut the cauliflower into bite-size florets.

3. **To make the batter:** In a bowl, mix together the flour, cornflour and salt. Gradually add the beer (or sparkling water) to form a batter the consistency of double (heavy) cream. You might not need to use all the liquid.

4. Heat the oil for deep-frying in a small saucepan.

5. Coat the florets in the batter. Fry in small batches for 3–4 minutes or until nicely golden and crisp. Lift out with a slotted spoon and drain on kitchen paper.

6. **To make the sauce:** Heat the oil in a wide non-stick frying pan. Add the garlic, chilli, ginger and white parts of the spring onions and stir-fry over a high heat for 30–50 seconds until fragrant and just tender (see picture below).

7. Add the water, light and dark soy sauces, vinegar and sugar, and bring to the boil. Add the fried florets and green parts of the spring onions (see picture overleaf).

8. Stir together for 30 seconds until the cauliflower is well coated. You can add a bit more light soy sauce or water if the sauce is too thick.

9. Serve at once with a salute to the general.

Gluten-free: Replace wheat flour with rice flour, use soda water and gluten-free soy sauces.

To bake: Arrange the coated florets on a baking tray (baking sheet) lined with parchment paper, drizzle each floret with some oil and bake in a preheated oven at Cauli**tip** 200°C (400°F/Gas 6) for 15 minutes until golden.

Thai cauliflower salad
Inspired by larb *gai*

On page 36 I described my love for tabbouleh salad, and I also love other herby salads from different cuisines worldwide. One of these salads hails from northern Thailand (and Laos) and is called *larb* (or *laab*). It contains minced meat and lots of fresh herbs, shallots, chillies and toasted rice.

During the time Adi and I spent in Thailand, we loved ordering this dish to see how it varies around the country. Later on I thought to myself: if cauliflower can work as a substitute for bulgur wheat, as in tabbouleh, could it replace meat in *larb*?

Since this recipe is in the book, you can guess the answer. Our star delivered, creating a super-fresh salad that got everyone who tried it excited.

In Thailand, every spicy salad is served with fresh cabbage or lettuce on the side – and from there I got the serving idea shown here. You can, of course, serve it in a bowl.

To save some preparation time, I replaced the ground toasted rice with chopped toasted peanuts.

serves 2–3 / contains fish / prep and cook: 15 minutes

Ingredients
1 small cauliflower
about 90 g (3 oz/small bunch) fresh coriander (cilantro)
leaves from 15–20 mint sprigs
leaves from 5–10 basil sprigs
1 small red onion or 2 shallots, peeled and finely chopped
2–3 spring onions (scallions), chopped
½ teaspoon dried chilli flakes (use less or more to your liking)
3–5 teaspoon Thai fish sauce
2–3 tablespoons freshly squeezed lime or lemon juice
½ teaspoon palm or brown sugar (whatever kind you have)
a handful of unsalted toasted peanuts, roughly chopped
leaves from 1–2 baby gem lettuce, to serve (optional)

Method
1. Cut the cauliflower into florets, then grate using a box grater into a large bowl.

2. Chop up all the herbs (not too finely). Add to the bowl of grated cauliflower along with the chopped onion or shallots, spring onion and chilli flakes.

3. Gently mix all the ingredients together, then season to taste with fish sauce, lime or lemon juice and sugar.

4. Add the peanuts and mix again. Serve at once, divided among lettuce leaves, if using.

Cauli**tip**

Vegan: Replace the fish sauce with light soy sauce or salt.

If you are not a coriander (cilantro) lover, omit it and use more of the other herbs.

Massaman curry
With baked cauliflower and potatoes

According to Thai food expert, Hanuman Aspler, of thaifoodmaster.com, *massaman* curry was created when Muslims from Persia started trading with some parts of seventeenth-century Siam.

They brought with them dry spices (like mace, nutmeg, cinnamon and cardamom) and added them into existing curry pastes, creating what is now known as the curry of Muslim people, a typical Thai dish loved by many.

In order to create the massaman curry paste, I added dried spices to a store-bought red curry paste. I used the Arabian baharat spice blend (read more about this on page 222), but garam masala works similarly well.

A typical *massaman* will contain meat (duck was my favourite in Thailand) and potatoes, and is topped with toasted peanuts or almonds. Our version contains oven-roasted cauliflower (that flourishes in the spicy environment) and potatoes.

serves 2–3 / contains fish / prep and cook: 1 hour

Ingredients
For the cauliflower and potatoes
1 small cauliflower, cut into medium-size florets
3 medium-size (unpeeled) potatoes, diced to 2.5 cm (1 in) cubes
2–3 tablespoons olive oil
fine sea salt

For the massaman curry paste
2 heaped tablespoons Thai red curry paste
1 teaspoon baharat spice blend or garam masala
¼ teaspoon ground turmeric
¼ teaspoon ground cumin
1 teaspoon olive oil or melted coconut oil

For the curry
1 tablespoon olive or coconut oil
2–3 tablespoons massaman curry paste (see above)
240 ml (8 fl oz/1 cup) full-fat coconut cream
120 ml (4 fl oz/1½ cup) water
2 dried or fresh kaffir lime leaves (optional)
1–2 star anise (optional)
1 tablespoon Thai fish sauce
leaves from 5 basil sprigs
1 teaspoon palm or brown sugar (whatever kind you have)
2–3 tablespoons toasted peanuts
steamed rice, to serve (page 142)

Method
1. Preheat the oven to 190°C (375°F/Gas 5).

2. **To make the cauliflower and potatoes:** Place the cauliflower and potatoes in a bowl. Add the oil and salt and toss to coat.

3. Arrange on a baking tray (baking sheet) lined with parchment paper and roast for 30 minutes until tender and golden. Set aside (see picture opposite).

4. **To make the curry paste:** Place all the paste ingredients in a small bowl and stir to combine.

5. **For the curry:** Heat the oil in a medium-size saucepan. Add the curry paste and fry over a medium-high heat for 30 seconds, or until fragrant. Gradually add the coconut cream 3–4 tablespoons at a time. Stir well to combine. Add the water and bring to the boil.

6. Add the kaffir lime, star anise, and fish sauce. Stir well.

7. Add the cauliflower and potatoes. If needed, add more coconut cream to the pan.

8. Bring to a strong boil and cook over a high heat for 1–2 minutes until the vegetables are warm through (it will smell so good). Add most of the basil leaves, remove from the heat and stir.

9. Taste and add more fish sauce and/or sugar to your liking.

10. Transfer to serving dishes, garnish with the remaining basil leaves and toasted peanuts, and serve with rice.

Vegan: Replace the fish sauce with light soy sauce or salt.

Don't like peanuts? Garnish with toasted almonds.

This is a mildly hot curry – add some chopped chillies or sriracha chilli sauce to spice things up.

Cauli**tip**

Stir-fried cauliflower rice
Without rice

How many times have you craved a stir-fry, but didn't feel like making rice or boiling noodles? Here the cauliflower bravely takes on a role once reserved only for carbs: acting as a bridge between an Asian sauce and a selection of vegetables, with everything cooked in one pan.

In my experience, grated cauliflower (using a box grater or with the help of the grating attachment of the food processor) delivers the best rice-like texture. But, you can use any technique to turn your cauliflower into 'grains' (see page 20).

There are quite a few cauli-rice recipes trending online. In my version, I used a combination of soy sauce, sugar and vinegar to get that Chinese restaurant flavour.

serves 3 / vegan / prep and cook: 20 minutes

Ingredients

For the stir-fry

1 small cauliflower
1 medium-size carrot, peeled
1 corncob or 100 g (4 oz/½ cup) frozen corn kernels
3–4 tablespoons olive oil
about 90 g (3 oz/large handful) frozen peas
1–2 spring onions (scallions), thinly sliced on the diagonal

For the sauce

3 tablespoons light soy sauce, to taste
2 tablespoons brown sugar (whatever kind you have), to taste
1 tablespoon vinegar, such as apple cider vinegar
 or rice wine vinegar

Method

1. **To make the stir-fry:** Cut the cauliflower into florets, then grate using a box grater into a large bowl.

2. Dice the carrot into small cubes. Remove the kernels from the corncob and separate them from each other.

3. Heat 2–3 tablespoons of the oil in a wide non-stick pan or wok.

4. When the oil is piping hot, add the grated cauliflower and stir-fry over a high heat for 2–3 minutes, until just tender and less pale. Stir vigorously (see picture opposite).

5. Remove the softened cauliflower and transfer to a bowl.

6. Allow the pan to reheat and add the remaining tablespoon of oil.

7. Add the peas, corn kernels and carrot. Stir-fry over a high heat 1–2 minutes, until just tender (see picture overleaf).

8. **To make the sauce:** Move all the vegetables to one side of the pan and add all the sauce ingredients. Stir over a high heat and bring to the boil to dissolve the sugar.

9. Once the sauce is bubbling fiercely, return the cauli-rice to the pan and stir well.

10. Taste and add more soy sauce and/or sugar to. Stir again (see picture overleaf).

11. Add most of the sliced spring onions and stir one last time.

12. Divide between serving plates and garnish with the remaining spring onions. Serve at once.

Gluten-free: Use gluten-free soy sauce.

Bell pepper, mushrooms, celery, onion and other vegetables can join this stir-fry – just make sure you cut them to small cubes.

Caulitip

Stir-fried cauliflower and broccoli
With mushrooms and (real) rice

Thailand's cities and towns are packed with lively night markets that serve some of the best street food in the world. During our stay in Chiang Mai, Adi and I visited such a market called Nimman night (next to the fancy MAYA centre). At one of the food stalls I ordered vegetable-packed stir-fried rice that inspired this dish.

Whenever stir-frying rice, it is best to use grains cooked the day before. Freshly made rice easily breaks apart. Thai jasmine rice is perfect here; fluffy basmati rice is too delicate in my opinion.

To save room on the hob, I steamed the cauliflower and broccoli in the microwave. Make sure not to discard the stems because they are both nutritious and delicious.

Since the recipe is made to feed four to five people, it is prepared in a shallow, wide pan rather than a saucepan. If you plan on making a smaller batch use a wide non-stick pan.

Like in Thailand, the rice is served with cucumbers that help refresh the palate between bites.

serves 4–5 / vegan / prep and cook: 1 hour

Ingredients

For the rice

185 g (6½ oz/1 cup) jasmine rice
360 ml (12½ fl oz/1½ cups) water

For the stir-fry

1 small cauliflower
1 small broccoli
about 240 g (8½ oz) mushrooms (preferably mixed,
 like chestnut and shimeji), roughly chopped
1 medium red onion, peeled and diced into 1½ cm (½ in) cubes
3–4 tablespoons oil

For the sauce

3–4 tablespoons light soy sauce, to taste
1–2 tablespoons brown sugar (whatever kind you have), to taste
1 teaspoon dark soy sauce

To serve

1 firm cucumber, sliced
1 small lemon or lime, cut into wedges
1–2 spring onions (scallions), thinly sliced

Method

1. **To cook the rice:** Place the rice in a fine sieve and rinse thoroughly in water. Drain well, then place in a small saucepan.

2. Add the water, bring to the boil over a high heat, then reduce the heat to low, cover and cook gently for 16 minutes until the rice is completely tender.

3. Remove from the heat and allow to rest for at least 10 minutes (preferably until completely cooled) before adding the rice to the stir-fry.

4. **To cook the cauliflower and broccoli:** Cut the broccoli and cauliflower into bite-size florets. Place in a large bowl and place the broccoli florets on top. Add enough water to come ¾ of the way up the cauliflower, cover with a plate and microwave for 3 minutes until just tender. Drain (see picture opposite).

5. Peel and thinly slice the broccoli stem.

6. **To cook the stir-fry:** Heat a shallow, wide pan over a high heat until piping hot for 2–3 minutes before you begin adding the ingredients. Add the oil, onion, broccoli stem and mushrooms. Fry, stirring constantly, for 2 minutes until the onion is just tender.

7. Add all steamed florets and stir-fry for 1 more minute. Add all the sauce ingredients, bring to the boil and stir well (see picture overleaf).

8. Add the cooled rice and stir well. Cook for 1 more minute, stirring constantly to allow the rice to warm through. Taste and add more soy sauce or sugar, if needed. If you see the rice sticking to the pot, add a little water and stir to loosen.

9. Divide onto serving plates, garnish each one with sliced cucumber, a lemon or lime wedge and some chopped spring onions and serve at once with your favourite hot sauce on the side.

Gluten-free: Use gluten-free soy sauce. If you can't find gluten-free dark soy sauce, simply omit it.

Cauli**tip**

Cauliflower pad ka pao
With Thai basil and crispy egg

Like *pad Thai* and red curry, *pad ka pao* (with different Latin spellings) is one of the Thai dishes that has most successfully been adopted by the West.

The most common versions contain minced beef or pork. But, many restaurants offer vegetable-based *pad ka paos*, and even the crispy fried egg commonly served with the dish can be omitted.

One day during our trip to Thailand, Adi and I went cycling in the rural part of the tranquil Pak Cong district. We stopped at a small restaurant on the side of the road. I watched a talented young cook (pictured right) prepare truly beautiful dishes that were simple yet elegant. My cauliflower *pad ka pao* is based on her technique.

For authentic results, use Thai basil, but ordinary basil will work in a pinch.

serves 2–3 / contains eggs / prep and cook: 20 minutes

Ingredients
For the stir-fry
1 small cauliflower
2–3 garlic cloves, peeled
½ fresh red chilli (use less or more to your liking)
3–4 tablespoons oil
5 tablespoons water
2 tablespoons light soy sauce, to taste
1 teaspoon dark soy sauce, to taste
1 teaspoon brown sugar (whatever kind you have), to taste
leaves from 8–10 basil sprigs (preferably Thai basil)

For Thai-style crispy fried eggs (optional)
2–3 medium eggs, (preferably free range)
4 tablespoons oil

To serve
steamed jasmine rice (see page 142)

Method
1. Cut the cauliflower into florets. Halve the florets lengthways, then cut, as if you were dicing, into pieces about the size of peanuts.

2. Thinly slice the garlic and chilli. Finely chop them to form a rough paste (this serves as a base for many Thai dishes).

3. Heat the oil in a wide non-stick pan.

4. Add the cauliflower and stir-fry for 1 minute. Add water, cover and let the cauliflower steam for another minute until just tender.

5. Remove the lid and allow the water to fully evaporate.

6. Move the cauliflower to one side of the pan, add some oil to the empty side and add the chopped chilli and garlic. Fry the chilli and garlic for 30 seconds, stirring, until fragrant. (see picture overleaf).

7. Add the soy sauces and sugar, and stir to dissolve. Stir the contents of the pan well, to coat the cauliflower with the sauce. Taste and add more soy sauce or sugar to taste. Add the basil leaves and stir-fry for 20 seconds until just wilted (see picture overleaf). Move to serving plates and serve with warm steamed rice and fried eggs, if you like.

8. **For the crispy fried eggs:** Heat the oil in a small saucepan over a high heat until it is slightly smoking. Crack in one egg and fry for 2–3 minutes, basting the yolk and top of the egg with hot oil. The egg is ready when the sides are golden and crisp, the white is fully opaque and the yolk is still soft and runny. Remove and repeat with the remaining eggs.

Vegan: Omit the fried egg.

Gluten-free: Use gluten-free soy sauce. If you can't find gluten-free dark soy sauce, omit it.

Caulitip

Lemon cauliflower
With chilli and sesame

When I was in junior high school, my mom would take me and my sisters to the local Chinese restaurant for lunch once a week. One of my favourite dishes there was crispy lemon chicken. Today I think of it as too sweet and syrupy, but it still brings back a lot of happy memories for me.

Inspired by the smashing success of General Tso's cauliflower (see page 130), I developed this very tasty cauliflower-based version of lemon chicken. I kept both the coating and the sauce delicate and simple. My sister even says she likes the cauli version more than the original dish!

If you try to coat raw florets with cornflour (cornstarch), it won't hold. But once steamed, the moisture released from the cauliflower just enough to allow for a fine coating.

serves 2–3 / vegan / prep and cook: 25 minutes

Ingredients
For the cauliflower
1 medium-size cauliflower
3 scant tablespoons cornflour (cornstarch)
¼ teaspoon sea salt
½ teaspoon baking powder
oil, for deep-frying

For the sauce
4 tablespoons freshly squeezed lemon juice (or more to your liking), to taste
2 scant tablespoons brown sugar (whatever kind you have), to taste
2 tablespoons light soy sauce

To serve
1 teaspoon white or whole sesame seeds
½ small lemon, thinly sliced
½ fresh red chilli, thinly sliced (use less or more to your liking)
1–2 spring onions (scallions), green part only, thinly sliced

Method
1. Toast the sesame seeds in a small, dry pan over a medium heat for 2–3 minutes, stirring, until fragrant and golden. Transfer to a plate and set aside.

2. **To cook the cauliflower:** Steam the cauliflower whole (see page 26) for 6–7 minutes, until the florets become just tender. Remove from the saucepan and let the cauliflower cool down a bit.

3. Cut the cauliflower into bite-size florets. Reserve the stem and leaves for other uses.

4. In a shallow bowl, mix the cornflour, salt and baking powder. Add the steamed florets and gently toss to coat finely.

5. **To cook the sauce:** Place lemon juice and sugar in a small saucepan and bring to a simmer over a medium-low heat. Allow the liquid to reduce by about ⅓, then add the soy sauce, taste and add more lemon juice, and/or sugar to taste. Remove from the heat.

6. Heat the oil for deep-frying in a small saucepan.

7. Fry the coated florets in small batches for 3–4 minutes, or until nicely golden. Lift out with a slotted spoon and drain on kitchen paper (see picture below).

8. Transfer the fried florets to a large bowl, pour over half the sauce and gently toss to coat. Taste and add more sauce, if desired. Any remaining sauce is great for stir-fries and keeps refrigerated for 3 months.

9. Serve the florets topped with sliced lemons, chilli and spring onions, then sprinkle with the toasted sesame seeds.

To bake: Lay the coated florets on a baking tray (baking sheet) lined with parchment paper, drizzle each floret with some oil and bake at 190 °C (375 °F/Gas 5) for 15 minutes until golden.

Add 3–4 drops of sesame oil to give the sauce a nutty richness.

Cauli**tip**   If you are making cauliflower steaks (see page 58) – use the trimmed florets to make this dish.

Pasta

Linguine with cauliflower ragu
Ready in under 30 minutes

The most popular ragu is *ragu alla bolognese*, which contains minced meat, wine and chopped vegetables. While most people associate the word with meaty sauces, ragu is actually a family of chunky sauces (rather than smooth, like tomato sauce, which is classified as *sugo*). Vegetarian ragu sauces may contain mushrooms, beetroot (beets), lentils, or, in our case: chopped cauliflower, proving light and fast to cook.

I chose to pair my take on ragu with linguine (little tongues in Italian) – the long and wide pasta that adheres well to the cauliflower. Short pasta shapes such as penne or farfalle also go well with this easy sauce.

Notice the use of the pasta cooking water in this dish. This is both seasoned and rich with starch, which is vital for thickening and enriching the sauce. It's the secret that makes the difference between a good and great pasta dish.

serves 2–3 / vegan / prep and cook: 25 minutes

Ingredients
about 30 g (1 oz/small handful) sliced almonds
1 small cauliflower
3–4 tablespoons olive oil
250 g (9 oz) pasta, such as linguine or farfalle
sea salt and freshly ground black pepper
4–5 tablespoons chopped chives or spring onions (scallions)
1 small lemon, cut into quarters (optional)

Method
1. Toast the almonds in a dry frying pan over a medium heat for 2–3 minutes, stirring, until lightly golden. Transfer to a plate and set aside to cool.

2. Cut the cauliflower into florets. Peel and roughly chop the main stem (reserving the other parts for other uses). Finely chop the florets and stem using a sharp knife (or you can grate or pulse in a food processor, see page 22).

3. Heat the olive oil in a wide pan. Add the cauliflower and sauté over a medium-high heat, stirring frequently, for 10–13 minutes until golden and tender.

4. Meanwhile, cook the pasta in a saucepan of well-salted boiling water for 1 minute less than recommended in the packet instructions. Drain and reserve 250–500 ml (9–18 fl oz/1–2 cups) of the cooking water.

5. Add the pasta to the pan with the cauliflower along with 120 ml (4 fl oz/½ cup) of the pasta water. Stir well and season to taste. Add most of the toasted almonds and the chopped chives and stir well to coat. Gradually add more water until the pasta is cooked to your liking.

6. To serve, divide the pasta among serving plates and garnish with the remaining almonds and chives.

Caulitip

Feel free to replace the almonds with any other nut you like: pistachios, pecans and even cashews will fit in quite nicely.

156

Cauliflower pasta Alfredo
More veg, less cream

During my childhood, my grandmother used to take my sisters and I on holidays in the city of Eilat. One of the things I loved about these holidays was the large breakfast buffet that always served potatoes with Alfredo sauce, and I wondered who this Alfredo guy was and what he was doing in our sauce.

Much later, I learnt that Alfredo was in fact a chef who owned a restaurant in Rome where would serve a pasta dish with butter and Parmesan. In 1920, two American actors ordered the dish and loved it so much that when they returned home, they coined the phrase 'pasta Alfredo' and helped turn it into a hit. Eventually, 'pasta Alfredo' became the generic term for cream sauce, including double (heavy) cream, mushrooms, prawns (shrimp), chicken and flour.

Because of cauliflower's ability to transform into a smooth cream when cooked, you get a much lighter sauce that helps increase your vegetable intake without compromising on flavour – win, win!

serves 4–5 / contains dairy / prep and cook: 30 minutes

Ingredients

For the sauce
1 medium-size cauliflower
30 g (1 oz/2 tablespoons) butter, diced (or more)
sea salt

For the pasta
500 g (1 lb 2 oz) pasta, such as wholewheat spaghetti, penne or fettuccine
4–5 tablespoons chopped chives, garlic chives or spring onions (scallions)
60 g (2 oz) Parmesan or aged Pecorino cheese
freshly ground white pepper (optional)

Method

1. **To make the sauce:** Cut the cauliflower into florets, then peel and roughly chop the main stem (reserving the stalks and leaves for making stock).

2. Place the florets and stem in a medium-size saucepan and just cover with water. Bring to the boil, then cook, uncovered, over a medium heat for 14–18 minutes until the florets are completely tender and easily mashed with a fork.

3. Remove about half the cooking liquid from the pan and set aside.

4. Add the butter and purée using a hand-held blender for 2–3 minutes or until you reach a very smooth, cream-like consistency, adding more cooking liquid if necessary.

5. Season the cauliflower cream with salt to taste (see picture opposite).

6. **To make the pasta:** Cook the pasta in a saucepan of well-salted water for 1 minute less than recommended on the packet instructions. Drain.

7. Using a vegetable peeler, shave the cheese to create delicate shavings.

8. Add the pasta to pan of cauliflower cream along with most of the chives and stir well. If the sauce feels to thick, thin it down with some of the cauliflower cooking liquid (see picture overleaf).

9. Cook for another 30 seconds. stirring frequently, or until the pasta is done to your liking and is well coated with the sauce. Taste and season with more salt and pepper if you wish.

10. To serve, transfer the pasta to serving plates and garnish with shaved Parmesan and the remaining chives.

Vegan: Replace the butter with 2 tablespoons of coconut oil or 80 ml (2 ½ fl oz/ ⅓ cup) of coconut cream.

Feel free to add 4–5 garlic cloves to the florets when you begin your cooking for a garlicky sauce.

Once the cream is ready, you can add cooked peas, sautéed mushrooms, tiny broccoli florets and more.

Caulitip

If you make a smaller amount of pasta, finish preparing the dish in a wide pan to control the amount of sauce.

Gnocchi, cauliflower and broccoli
In pesto cream sauce

Whenever Assaf Ambram is not busy taking beautiful photographs of food, such as the ones in this book, he likes cooking at home for his wife, Liron, and their two kids. When I told him that I was planning to include a pasta chapter in this book, he told me that this dish is one of his specialities: fast, easy and really delicious.

While store-bought herb pesto works just fine here, it's even better when you make it yourself. See page 176 for a tasty coriander (cilantro) pesto (replace with basil if you prefer).

serves 2–3 / contains dairy / prep and cook: 15 minutes

Ingredients
1 small head of broccoli
½ small cauliflower
500 g (1 lb 2 oz) high-quality potato gnocchi
3 tablespoons olive oil
4 garlic cloves, peeled and thinly sliced
180 ml (6 fl oz/¾ cup) double (heavy) cream or single (light) cream
1 heaped tablespoon basil or herb pesto (see page 176)
sea salt and freshly ground black pepper

Method
1. Cut the broccoli and cauliflower into bite-size florets – about the size of the gnocchi.

2. Cook the gnocchi in a saucepan of boiling salted water according to the instructions on the packet. Strain and reserve the cooking water.

3. Heat the oil in a wide frying pan. Add the garlic and fry for 30 seconds over a medium heat, until fragrant and slightly soft but not golden.

4. Add the cauliflower florets, 1–2 ladles of the reserved cooking water and the cream. Bring to the boil over high heat and cook 1 minute.

5. Add the broccoli florets and cook for another minute over a high heat until slightly tender but still retaining a little bite. Add more gnocchi water if you feel the sauce is too thick.

6. Add the cooked gnocchi and pesto and stir well until the sauce takes on a vibrant green colour and the gnocchi are well coated. If the sauce doesn't coat the gnocchi well, simply cook for another minute to thicken.

7. Season generously with salt and pepper, and serve.

Vegan and lactose-free: Replace the cream with full-fat coconut cream.

Gluten-free: Use gluten-free gnocchi.

Cauli**tip**

Cauliflower mac and cheese
Topped with golden cauliflower crumbs

One of my favourite things to eat as a child was packet mac and cheese, with all the funky pasta shapes and the powdered sauce (that I hope contained some actual cheese).

When I started cooking at home as a teenager, I began making it from scratch; it wasn't so hard and tasted a lot better than my childhood memories of the packet stuff. I remember feeling so proud seeing my family devouring the pasta from the piping hot pan.

My twist on this comfort food classic replaces the regular breadcrumbs with hand-chopped cauliflower bits. They brown up really nicely, and add another layer of cauliflower to the florets in the pan.

serves 6 (makes a 25 cm/10 in square pan) / contains dairy / prep and cook: 1¼ hours

Ingredients

For the pasta

1 medium-small cauliflower
350 g (12 oz) short pasta, such as fusilli, penne or elbows
2 tablespoons olive oil
1 heaped tablespoon sea salt (for seasoning the pasta water)

For the béchamel sauce

30 g (1 oz, 2 tablespoons) butter
1 heaped tablespoons plain (all-purpose) flour
480 ml (16 fl oz/2 cups) full-fat (whole) milk
150 g (5 oz/½ cup) Gouda cheese, grated
150 g (5 oz/½ cup) white or orange Cheddar cheese, grated
1/4 teaspoon freshly grated nutmeg (optional)
sea salt and coarsely ground black pepper

Method

1. Preheat the oven to 190°C (375°F/Gas 5).

2. Cut the cauliflower into large florets. Set 2–3 florets aside and cut the rest into bite-size pieces.

3. **To make the pasta and cauliflower:** Cook the pasta in a saucepan of boiling, salted water for 5 minutes less than recommended on the packet instructions. Add the bite-size florets and cook for another 4 minutes, until both the pasta and florets are tender but still retaining a little bite. Drain, rinse with cold water and transfer to a large bowl.

4. **To make the béchamel sauce:** Melt the butter in a medium saucepan over a high heat. Add the flour and stir vigorously for a minute or so until a thick paste forms. Reduce the heat to medium, add one-third of the milk and bring to the boil, stirring.

5. Add the rest of the milk and return to the boil, stirring. Simmer for 1–2 minutes over a low heat until the sauce is thick enough to coat the back of a spoon. Remove from the heat.

6. Blend in the cheeses. Taste and add salt if necessary (but remember the cheeses are quite salty). Add the nutmeg, if using, and pepper and stir.

7. Pour the sauce over the pasta and cauliflower and stir gently. Transfer to an oiled ovenproof pan or parchment-paper-lined pan (see picture overleaf).

8. Finely chop or grate the florets set aside earlier. Add the oil (directly onto the cutting board) and mix to coat, then sprinkle over the contents of the pan (see picture below).

9. Bake in the oven for 20–30 minutes, until the cauliflower crumbs are golden and the smell is irresistible. Serve hot, alongside a fresh green salad.

Caulitip

Gluten-free: Replace the plain (all-purpose) flour in the sauce with chickpea (garbanzo) or potato flour, and use gluten-free pasta.

Vegan: Replace the béchamel with 600 ml (21 fl oz/2 ½ cups) of cauliflower cream (see page 35) mixed with 1 tablespoon of beer yeast or miso paste.

Experiment with other cheeses like Mozzarella or Kashkaval cheese.

Out of the oven

Cauliflower pizza
Gluten-free

My first professional job in the culinary world was as a pizza maker in a small Italian restaurant. You can imagine my astonishment when cauliflower pizza clips and recipes started trending online – which replace the centuries-old yeast dough with a blitzed cauliflower and egg crust.

The paleo recipes I tested were completely carb-free and pulled away nicely, but felt too patty-like. So, I tried adding cornflour (cornstarch) to my crust, and it made the end result more stable and crunchy on the sides.

Feel free to play around with the toppings – mushrooms, onions and peppers, feta cheese and fresh mozzarella are worthy additions to your pizza.

serves 3 / contains dairy and eggs / gluten-free / prep and cook: 1 hour

Ingredients

1 medium-size cauliflower
2 scant tablespoons cornflour (cornstarch)
30 g (1 oz) Pecorino or Parmesan cheese, grated
sea salt, to taste
2 medium-size eggs, preferably free-range
fine sea salt and freshly ground black pepper

For the sauce

200 g (7 oz/small can) whole tinned tomatoes
½ teaspoon dried oregano (optional)
½ teaspoon garlic powder

Toppings

100 g (3 ½ oz/½ cup) mozzarella cheese, grated
1 small red onion, peeled and thinly sliced
a handful of pitted black olives, sliced
leaves from 1–2 basil sprigs, to garnish

Method

1. Preheat the oven to 180°C (350°F/Gas 4) and line a baking tray (baking sheet) with parchment paper.

2. Cut the cauliflower into even-sized florets. Place in the bowl of a food processor and pulse 6–7 times until you reach a consistency similar to fine breadcrumbs (grating the florets also works).

3. Move the cauli-crumbs to a wide, dry, non-stick pan. Cook over a high heat for 6–8 minutes, stirring. The crumbs will emit steam and moisture we don't want on our crust. When the crumbs are tender they are ready to go. It's OK if some crumbs become golden (See picture opposite).

4. Transfer to a bowl and allow to cool for 3–4 minutes.

5. Add the cornflour (cornstarch), grated cheese and salt to taste and stir well.

6. Crack in one egg and stir to combine. Beat the second egg in another bowl. If the mixture feels dry and crumbly, gradually add the beaten egg until you can mould the

mixture with your hand without it crumbling.

7. Place on the prepared baking tray and flatten into a 1 cm (½ in) thick circle (see picture overleaf).

8. Bake for 18–22 minutes until the sides are slightly golden and the crust feels firm to the touch.

9. **To make the sauce:** Place the tomatoes in a blender and purée until smooth. Add the oregano (if using) and garlic powder and season with salt and pepper to taste.

10. **To create the pizza:** Ladle 1–2 scoops of the sauce on the baked crust. Spread evenly, leaving a (2 cm/¾ in) border (see picture overleaf).

11. Sprinkle over the mozzarella and top with the sliced onion and olives. Return to the oven and bake for a further 10 minutes, or until the cheese is bubbly.

12. Remove, sprinkle over the basil leaves and serve at once.

Paleo: Omit the cornflour (cornstarch).

Vegan: Replace the eggs with 2 heaped tablespoons of chia seeds, soaked overnight with 120 ml (4 fl oz/1/2 cup) of water. Top with cashew cheese.

Cauli**tip**   Use any excess tomato sauce for pasta dishes.

Pumpkin and cauliflower pash'tida
Jewish crustless pie

Pash'tida is a Hebrew word that describes a family of savoury baked goods. It was very popular in Israel during the 1970s. Reminiscent of a quiche without the crust and with soft cheeses added to it, *pash'tida* was the recipe to pull out whenever you had some leftovers and wanted to revive them.

Though not as trendy now, it still holds a nostalgic spot for most Israelis.

For this recipe, I took a traditional *pash'tida* batter and upgraded it with sliced cauliflower and diced sweet pumpkin. If you are not a pumpkin fan, use a sweet potato or diced bell pepper.

serves 5–6 / contains eggs and dairy / prep and cook: 30 minutes

Ingredients

olive oil or melted butter, to grease the pan
½ small cauliflower
250 g (9 oz) cottage cheese
150 g (5 oz/⅔ cup) natural yoghurt, 3 per cent fat or more
about ½ teaspoon sea salt
5 tablespoons oatmeal or breadcrumbs
½ teaspoon baking powder
5 medium or 4 large eggs, preferably free-range
4–5 dill (or parsley) sprigs, finely chopped
250 g (8 oz) slice of pumpkin, peeled and diced into small cubes

Method

1. Preheat the oven to 180°C (350°F/Gas 4). Oil or butter a 20 cm (8 in) cake pan.

2. Cut the cauliflower into florets, then thinly slice the florets.

3. Place the cheese, yoghurt, salt, oatmeal and baking powder in a bowl. Crack in the eggs and stir to combine. Fold in the cauliflower, pumpkin and dill.

4. Pour the mixture to the prepared pan. Bake for 45–55 minutes until golden and set; a knife inserted in the centre should come out clean.

5. Remove from the oven, allow to cool and serve. Keeps refrigerated for up to 5 days.

Cauli tip

Gluten-free: Replace the oats and bread crumbs in the pie with chickpea (gram) flour.

Paleo: Replace the oats and bread crumbs with 1 grated potato, well squeezed.

Vegan: Replace the eggs and dairy with 330 g (11 oz/1⅓ cups) silken tofu mashed with 4 tablespoons of chickpea (gram) flour, 1 teaspoon of miso paste and 4 tablespoons of water.

Puff pastry khachapuri
Filled with cauliflower and onion

Tbilisi-born chef Irma Kazar is known locally as the expert on all things having to do with Georgian food. As a cooking instructor and pastry chef, she encourages home cooks to embrace the wonderful and rich cuisine she grew up on.

Khachapuri is one of Georgia's typical pastries – usually boat-shaped and filled with cheese. When Irma told me she had a quick cauliflower *khachapuri* to share, I knew it had to be in the book. She even agreed to join us on set, so we could document how to make the beautiful parcel shape.

This pastry is usually made with yeast leavened dough (or laminated homemade dough), and our small cheat is to use good-quality store-bought puff pastry, placed in the fridge to defrost slowly overnight.

To accompany the pastries, we prepared herb pesto with a delicious Georgian twist: coriander (cilantro) leaves join the basil, and walnuts replace the pine nuts.

makes 12 pastries / contains egg and dairy (depending on the dough) / prep and cook: 1½ hours

Ingredients

For the filling

1 small cauliflower
4 tablespoons olive oil
2 medium-size onions, peeled and diced into small cubes
60 ml (2 fl oz/¼ cup) water
1 teaspoon dried coriander (cilantro) leaves (optional)
35 g (1¾ oz/⅓ cup) shelled walnuts, coarsely chopped
sea salt and freshly ground black pepper

For the khachapuri

2–3 tablespoons flour, for dusting
300 g (1 lb 2 oz) good-quality puff pastry (preferably butter-based), defrosted if frozen
1 medium-size egg, preferably free-range, beaten

For the pesto

about 60 g (2 oz/1/2 bunch) coriander (cilantro), chopped
1 garlic clove, peeled and sliced
leaves from 6–8 basil sprigs
30 g (1 oz/¼ cup) shelled walnuts
60 ml (2 fl oz/¼ cup) olive oil
1 teaspoon freshly squeezed lemon juice (optional)

Method

1. Preheat the oven to 180°C (350°F/Gas 4) and line a baking tray (baking sheet) with parchment paper.

2. **To make the filling:** Cut the cauliflower into florets, then chop with a knife into peanut-size pieces (reserve leaves and stems for stock, see page 22).

3. Heat the oil in a wide frying pan. Add the onions and cook over a medium heat for 10–14 minutes, stirring, until they are lightly golden. Add the cauliflower and cook for a further 6 minutes, until just tender.

4. Add the water, bring to the boil and cook over a medium-low heat, uncovered, for 5–7 minutes until the cauliflower is tender and all the water has evaporated. Remove from the heat.

5. Stir in the dried coriander and chopped walnuts, season with salt and pepper and stir. Allow to cool for 10 minutes (transfer to a bowl if you like).

6. **To make the pastries:** Roll out the dough on a floured work surface to 5 mm (¼ in) thick, then cut into 12 even squares. Place 1–2 tablespoons of the filling in the centre of each square. (see picture below).

7. Hold a square by two diagonal corners. Lift one and lay over the filling, place the other on top and press the corners with your fingers to tighten. Lift and press the other corners similarly to create a square parcel (see picture overleaf).

8. Transfer the parcels to the prepared baking tray and brush with the beaten egg. Bake for 13–15 minutes until risen, golden and crisp.

9. **To make the pesto:** Meanwhile, place all the pesto ingredients in a blender and pulse to form a paste. Taste and season to your liking, adding the lemon juice if you like.

10. Serve the khachapuris along with the pesto.

Vegan: Omit the egg, use oil-based puff pastry

You can replace the dried coriander (cilantro) leaves with a scant teaspoon of ground coriander seeds.

Cauli**tip**

Cauliflower kubbeh sini'ye
With onion and mushrooms in a bulgur wheat crust

Think of *kubbeh sini'ye* as the Arabian shepherd's pie. It is made in a metal pan (called a sini'ye) it is usually filled with spicy minced beef or lamb in a crunchy bulgur wheat crust, much easier to make than the typical fried kubbeh of the Levant.

In my vegetarian *kubbeh sini'ye* the mighty cauliflower is used twice: in the filling, where it is firstly cooked with onions, mushrooms and baharat (see page 224), then once in the crust.

The crust calls for using fine bulgur wheat. Bulgur wheat is whole-wheat grains, that have been cooked, dried and crushed to various sizes. Coarse bulgur wheat needs about 15 minutes of cooking, while fine bulgur wheat is so small – it only needs a soak in cold water to rehydrate and become edible. It is available in some supermarkets and Middle Eastern stores, and you can order it online.

If you can't find the right bulgur wheat, that's OK. Top your dish with a large batch of homemade tahini (see page 38) and bake for 10-15 minutes until golden. This is another dish, called *sini'ye bet'hina*.

serves 6 (makes a 20 x 30 cm/8 x 12 in pan) / vegan / prep and cook: 1¼ hours

Ingredients

For the crust

275 g (10 oz/1½ cups) fine bulgur wheat
350 ml (12 fl oz/½ cup) water
4 tablespoons plain (all-purpose) or wholewheat flour
2 tablespoons tomato purée (paste)
1/2 teaspoon fine sea salt
80 ml (2½ fl oz/⅓ cup) olive oil

For the filling

1 medium-size cauliflower
5 tablespoons olive oil
2 medium-size onions, peeled and diced into cubes
500 g (1 lb 2 oz) chestnut mushrooms, coarsely chopped
180 ml (6 fl oz/¾ cup) water
1 teaspoon baharat (or garam masala or ras el hanut)
sea salt and freshly ground black pepper

Method

1. Preheat the oven to 210°C (425°F/Gas 6) and have ready a 20 x 30 cm (8 x 12 in) pan.

2. **To make the crust:** Place the bulgur wheat and water in a bowl, stir and set aside for 1 hour to soak (the bulgur should absorb all of the water).

3. **To make the filling:** Cut the cauliflower into florets. Set 4–6 florets aside for the crust, cut the remaining florets into bite-size pieces (see picture overleaf).

4. Heat the oil in a medium-size saucepan. Add the onions and cook over a high heat for 6–8 minutes until translucent, stirring occasionally. Add the cauliflower and mushrooms and cook for a further 8 minutes, still stirring, until just tender.

5. Add the water and cook, uncovered, over a high heat for 6–8 minutes until the cauliflower is tender and the water has completely evaporated. Season with baharat, salt and pepper to taste. Spoon into the prepared pan (see picture overleaf).

6. **Return to the crust**: Add the flour, tomato purée and salt to the soaked bulgur. Knead for 1 minute to form a dough. Flatten the dough on top of the vegetables (see picture overleaf).

7. Halve the reserved florets lengthways and place in rows pressing into the crust. Using a small knife, cut the crust around the florets to portion out servings (see picture overleaf).

8. Drizzle the crust generously with oil (see Caulitip below). Bake for 20–25 minutes until the crust turns golden and crisp. Remove from the oven and serve at once (see picture below).

9. The kubbeh sini'ye keeps refrigerated for up to 3 days and is best warmed up in a hot oven or toaster oven.

Caulitip

If you have any cooked lentils (see page 40) or other beans, add about 200 g (7 oz/ 1 cup) to the filling.

The more generous you are with the olive oil when drizzling the dish before baking, the crispier the crust will get.

Spinach and cauliflower filo pie
Spanakopita goes vegan

The ancient cuisine of Greece and its islands has always fascinated me. I think it is something about the philosophy that puts an the emphasis on simple ingredients, minimum fuss and maximum flavour. My three trips to the Greek islands were memorable, and left a huge impact on the way I cook at home.

You know how inspiration can come out of nowhere? One day I was preparing a batch of spinach and cauliflower for a *shakshooka* (see page 208). The batch turned out way larger than I needed, then I realised: this mixture can turn into a great filling!

The texture of the spinach and cauliflower reminded me of the *spanakopitas* (spinach and feta cheese pies) I had in Greece, and in a matter of days the idea turned into a new way to fill a filo pie, which vegans and those who are lactose intolerant can enjoy equally.

Here the cauliflower plays a supportive role, adding texture and character to the robust, green spinach. Along with some olives and fragrant dill, you get a comforting crispy pie that will surely remind you of your time in Greece (or make you want to get on the first plane).

serves 6 (makes a 20 x 30 cm/ 8 x 12 in pan) / vegan / prep and cook: 1½ hours

Ingredients

For the filling

1 small cauliflower
4 tablespoons olive oil, plus extra for greasing
60 ml (2 fl oz/¼ cup) water
500 g (1 lb 2 oz) fresh spinach leaves, roughly chopped if large
8–12 kalamata olives, pitted and chopped
4–8 dill sprigs, finely chopped
2 tablespoons chickpea (gram) flour or breadcrumbs
fine sea salt and freshly ground black pepper

For the filo layers

1 packet frozen filo sheets (250–270 g/8–9 oz/ 7 large sheets), defrosted
80 ml (2½ fl oz/⅓ cup) olive oil

Method

1. Preheat the oven to 180°C (350°F/Gas 4) and grease a 30 x 20 cm (12 x 8 in) pan with oil.

2. **To make the filling:** Cut the cauliflower into florets, then slice them thinly (reserving the other parts for stock, see page 24).

3. Heat the 4 tablespoons of oil in a shallow wide pan. Add the sliced cauliflower and sauté over a high heat for 6–7 minutes, stirring frequently, until just tender and golden.

4. Add the water, bring to the boil, cover and cook over a high heat for a further 5 minutes, until tender. Add the spinach and stir well. Cook for 3 minutes, stirring occasionally, until the leaves have wilted and lost most of their volume (see picture opposite).

5. Transfer to a colander and set inside a large bowl and allow to cool slightly.

6. When cooled enough to handle, firmly squeeze the spinach and cauliflower to get rid of excess liquid. Discard the liquid

in the bowl and place the vegetables inside.

7. Add the olives, dill and the chickpea (gram) flour or breadcrumbs. Mix to combine and season with salt and pepper (note that the olives are salty).

8. **To make the pie:** Brush one filo sheet all over with oil and place in the pan. Fold in the edges of the sheet. Brush a second sheet and lay on the first sheet, leaving the sides of the sheet on the sides of the pan. Repeat with 2 more sheets (see pictures overleaf).

9. Lay the filling mixture in the pan and flatten (see pictures overleaf).

10. Lay 3 more oiled sheets on top of the filling, allowing the sides to overhang the sides of the pan (see picture overleaf).

11. Bake for 18–22 minutes, until nicely golden. Remove from the oven and serve at once.

The filling mixture can be used to fill other pastry goods, from empanadas to samosas.

Caulitip   For easy serving, cut to portions with a small knife before baking.

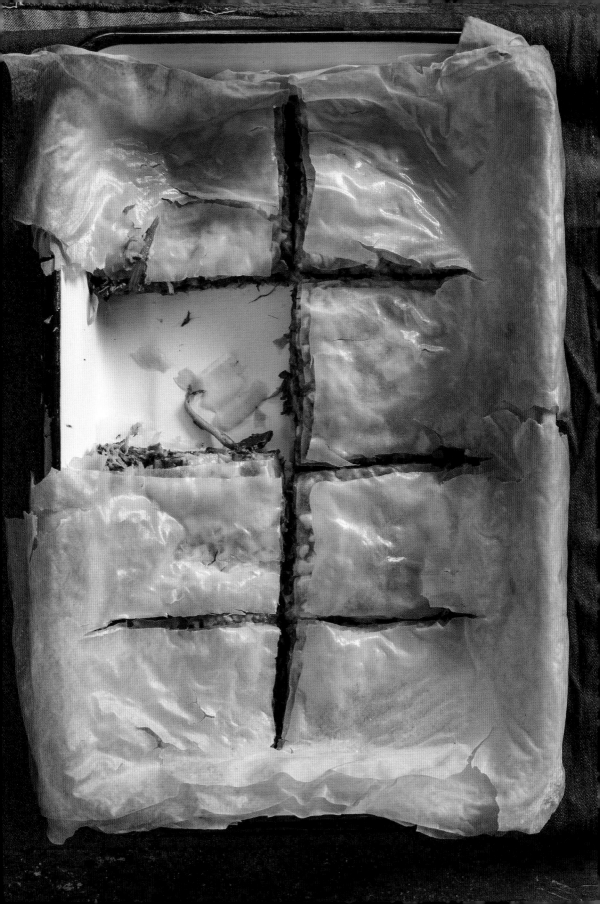

My lil' cookie
Savoury Parmesan cookies with caramelised cauliflower

At the beginning of the book I stated that one of my goals is to make caramelised cauliflower a thing, and here is one creative way you can use it.

These savoury cookies are an irresistible snack, and great for entertaining. They are based on a recipe by the gifted baking blogger Natalie Levin (lilcookie.com), that originally contained nuts, but now contains cauliflower instead. It does require more work, but you will be rewarded with a truly remarkable bite.

You can incorporate the leftover cauliflower from this recipe into the quiche dough (see page 196) or in the Alfredo pasta sauce (see page 158).

makes 50–60 cookies / contains dairy / prep and cook: 3 hours

Ingredients

For the caramelised cauliflower

1 medium-size cauliflower
1/2 teaspoon sea salt
80 ml (3 fl oz/⅓ cup) olive oil

For the cookies

120 g (4 oz) butter, softened
60 g (2 oz) Parmesan cheese, grated
30 g (1 oz) cream cheese
¼ teaspoon sea salt (optional)
125 g (4 oz/1 cup) all-purpose, spelt or gluten-free flour
¼ teaspoon freshly ground black pepper
4 tablespoons poppy seeds (optional)

Method

1. **To make the caramelised cauliflower:** Cut the cauliflower into florets, then chop them into pieces resembling breadcrumbs (using a food processor, a box grater or knife). Transfer the florets to a wide pan, then add the salt and oil. Cook over a medium-high heat, stirring frequently, for 9–13 minutes until golden (not brown).

2. Pour the contents of the pan into a fine sieve set over a small bowl (discard or re-use the oil).

3. **To make the cookie dough:** Place the butter, Parmesan and cream cheese in a medium-size bowl and mix well. Add 2 heaped tablespoons of the caramelised cauliflower and stir. Taste and add salt if necessary. Add the flour and black pepper and mix to combine.

4. Form the dough into two 4 cm (1½ in) logs. Roll on a floured or poppy seed (if using) covered surface. Move to a plate or tray, cover with cling film (plastic wrap) and chill for 2 hours or freeze for 1 hour until firm.

5. Preheat the oven to 160°C (325 °F/Gas 3) and line a large baking tray (baking sheet) with parchment paper. Cut the logs into 5 mm (¼ in) thick coins. Place on the prepared baking tray and bake for 10–12 minutes until golden. Allow to cool before munching begins.

Sweet potato and potato gratin
With cauliflower cream and thyme

The French potato gratin played an important role in my culinary evolution. Nine years ago I was working in a book shop. After watching chef Bobby Flay prepare a sweet potato gratin on *Iron Chef America*, I scanned some cookbooks in the store until I found a recipe, and then went home and made it for my family.

They were so impressed, it made me realise that the world of food was perhaps worth further exploration. Although I have made many of gratin dishes since, I'm still excited to serve it every time.

After shooting the crown soup (see page 106) I came home with some of the leftover cauliflower cream. I had some potatoes on hand and figured I could repeat the move I made with the pasta Alfredo dish (see page 158). And it worked! You can slice the potatoes in any way you see fit: with a sharp knife, a mandolin or with the slicing attachment of your food processor.

For a dairy-filled version, replace the coconut cream for double (heavy) cream and top the dish with a big handful of grated parmesan on step 7 – before baking.

serves 5-6 (makes a 25 cm/10 in round pan) / vegan / gluten-free / prep and cook: 2 hours

Ingredients

For the cream
1 small cauliflower
500 ml (17 fl oz/2 cups) coconut cream
sea salt

For the gratin
2 medium-size sweet potatoes, peeled and thinly sliced
3 medium-large potatoes, peeled and thinly sliced
leaves from 10 thyme sprigs
ground white pepper, to taste

Method

1. Preheat the oven to 180°C (350°F/Gas 4).

2. **To make the cream:** Cut the cauliflower into bite-sized florets. Peel and roughly chop the main stem. Place the florets and stem in a medium-size saucepan and add just enough water to cover. Bring to the boil over a high heat, then cook, uncovered, over a medium heat for 16–18 minutes until the florets are completely tender.

3. Remove about half of the cooking liquid and set aside. Add the coconut cream and purée using a hand-held blender for 2–3 minutes or until very smooth, adding more cooking liquid if necessary. Season with salt to taste.

4. Place the potatoes and sweet potatoes in a large bowl. Add the thyme leaves and 500 ml (17 fl oz/2 cups) of the cream. Season with salt and pepper and mix well.

5. Move the contents of the bowl to a pan and flatten to form layers. The cream should reach the height of the potatoes.

6. Cover the pan with parchment paper and seal with kitchen foil. Bake for about 1 hour until the slices are completely tender – check with a fork, and be wary of the hot steam when taking off the foil and paper.

7. Remove the covers and bake for a further 15 minutes or until the top is lightly golden. Remove and serve.

Cauliflower ma'akooda
The North African frittata

Ma'akooda is a lovely north African pie, similar in method to that of an Italian frittata and Spanish tortilla. It is an egg-based dish with mashed potatoes, loaded with herbs and coloured with a pinch of turmeric.

Like its European parallels, the *ma'akooda* can be filled with a variety of vegetables. Peas and fresh broad (fava) beans are delicious choices in the spring, and peppers and aubergines (eggplants) in summer. Winter is the season for cauliflower and for me, it makes the best filling – especially when you cut into the pie and see the florets studded inside like glittering jewels.

Some home cooks like to steam or boil the florets (3–4 minutes until just tender) before adding them to the batter, but I like to add them uncooked because I like to retain their texture.

If the cauliflower leaves and stalks are nice and vibrant – finely chop and add them to the batter as well.

serves 6-8 / gluten-free / contains eggs / prep and cook: 1 hour

Ingredients

3 medium-size potatoes (skin on)
4–6 tablespoons olive oil
1 medium-size onion, peeled and diced into medium-size cubes
about 75 g (2½ oz/1 small bunch) parsley (including the stems)
2–3 spring onions (scallions), both white and green parts
1 small cauliflower
1/2 teaspoon ground turmeric (you can use a bit more for a stronger yellow colour)
6–8 large eggs, preferably free-range, beaten
1 teaspoon sea salt
freshly ground black pepper

Method

1. Preheat the oven to 180°C (350°F/Gas 4).

2. **To cook the potatoes:** In a small saucepan of boiling water, cook the potatoes for 30–40 minutes until completely soft. Alternatively, place the potatoes in a microwave-safe bowl with 120 ml (4 fl oz/½ cup) of water, cover and microwave for 12–15 minutes until soft.

3. Carefully remove the skin from the potatoes while still hot. Transfer to a large bowl and mash the potatoes using a fork or potato masher. Allow the mash to cool slightly (see picture opposite).

4. Heat the oil in an ovenproof, wide shallow pan (preferably non-stick), add the onion and sauté over a high heat for 4–5 minutes until just tender.

5. **To make the batter:** Meanwhile, cut the spring onions (scallions) into tiny rings and finely chop the parsley. Cut the cauliflower into medium-small florets.

6. Add the herbs, turmeric and salt and pepper to the bowl of mashed potatoes.

7. Add the eggs to the potatoes and stir to form a batter. Stir the florets in gently.

8. Pour the batter over the onions. Cook over a medium heat for 3–4 minutes, until the sides are beginning to set.

9. Transfer to the oven (uncovered) and bake for 15–20 minutes until completely set in the centre (a knife inserted should come out clean).

10. Carefully remove from the oven, allow to cool for 10 minutes, then place a large plate on top and even more carefully turn over to release from the pan (see picture overleaf).

11. Allow the ma'akooda to cool down a bit before cutting into wedges and serving warm.

Vegan: Replace the eggs with 400 g (14 oz/1 1/2 cups) silken tofu mashed or blitzed with 6 tablespoons of chickpea (gram) flour and 120 ml (4 fl oz/1/2 cup water). The vegan ma'akooda must be cooled completely before turning out of the pan.

Cauli**tip**

Cauliflower and pistachio quiche
Inspired by a trip to Provence

While travelling with Adi near the lavender fields of Provence, we decided to have a light lunch in the town of Manosque. We found a small café that served a wide variety of quiches: one with cherry tomatoes and aubergines (eggplants), one with pears and blue cheese and one with pistachios and roasted cauliflower – so memorable I can still taste the crunchy crust and creamy filling.

I used wholewheat flour for the crust in this quiche. It's worth knowing that when making shortcrust pastries, wholewheat can replace the plain white flour without any modification to the recipe.

serves 5-6 (makes a 25 cm/10 in round springform cake pan) / contains eggs and dairy / prep and cook: 2½ hours

Ingredients

For the dough

250 g (9 oz/2 cups) wholewheat flour, plus extra for dusting
½ teaspoon fine salt
120 g (4 oz) butter, softened or olive oil
1 medium-size egg, preferably free-range
1-4 tablespoons cold water

For the cauliflower and filling

1 medium-small cauliflower
3-4 tablespoons olive oil
100 g (3⅓ oz) grated gouda, Cheddar or monterey jack
 cheese
60 g (2 oz) feta cheese
handful of shelled pistachios
fine sea salt and freshly ground black pepper

For the royale

250 ml (9 fl oz/1 cup) double (heavy) cream
125 ml (4 fl oz/½ cup) single (light) cream
2 tablespoons wholewheat flour
3 medium-size eggs, preferably free-range
sea salt and freshly ground black pepper

Method

1. Preheat the oven to 190°C (375°F/Gas 5)

2. **To make the dough:** Sift the flour in a large bowl. Add the salt and rub in the butter or oil until you have a soft breadcrumb-like texture. Add the egg and enough cold water to make the mixture come together to form a dough.

3. Roll out the dough on a floured surface to 1 cm (½ in) thick. Grab pieces of the dough and use them to tile the pan with an even layer of dough (without any holes), coming up the sides of the pan to about 5 cm (2 in). Freeze for 1 hour while preparing the filling.

4. **To cook the cauliflower:** Steam the cauliflower whole (see page 26) for 10 minutes or until just tender. Transfer to a large bowl, allow to cool slightly, then cut into medium-size

florets. Roughly chop the main stem of the cauliflower.

5. Place the florets and stem in a large bowl, add the oil and salt and pepper to taste and toss gently to coat. Put them on a baking tray (baking sheet) lined with parchment paper. Bake in the oven for 15–20 minutes until the florets are golden. Remove and allow to cool slightly.

6. Adjust the oven temperature to 180°C (350°F/Gas 4) and lightly grease the pan.

7. **To prepare the royale:** Whisk together the creams, flour and eggs in a bowl to combine. Season with salt and pepper.

8. **To assemble the quiche:** Lay the baked florets and stem on the frozen dough. Scatter the grated cheese on top. Pour over the royale and gently shake the pan so the filling reaches every corner. Crumble over the feta and sprinkle with the pistachios (see picture below).

9. Bake for about 45 minutes, or until the dough is golden and the filling is set (a knife inserted in the centre should come out clean).

10. Remove from the oven and allow to cool down to room temperature before extracting from the pan and serving. Keeps refrigerated for about 4 days.

Vegan: See the vegan appendix to the book online: https://goo.gl/ndJp7m

Walnuts, pecans and pine nuts can replace the pistachios.

Cauli**tip**

From the hob

Braised cauliflower greens
In lemon and garlic

Unlike spinach or Swiss chard, cauliflower greens don't give into heat quickly, and require a long cooking time. In the US they are cooked for a long time with various spices, along with mustard and broccoli greens, and served as a typical side dish for barbecued meat.

For this recipe I braise them the Mediterranean way, with a lot of garlic and fresh lemon juice.

To get your hands on some large greens, get in touch with a farmer – many will deliver them straight from the field.

serves 3 / vegan / gluten-free / paleo / prep and cook: 50 minutes

Ingredients
10–12 large cauliflower leaves, well rinsed
4–5 tablespoons olive oil
8–10 garlic cloves, peeled and sliced
60 ml (4 fl oz/¼ cup) water
4–5 tablespoons freshly squeezed lemon juice
sea salt and freshly ground black pepper

Method
1. Separate the leafy greens from the white stalks. Reserve the stalks for making stock (see page 24). Cut the leaves into 1 cm (½ in) thick strips.

2. Bring a medium saucepan of water to the boil. Add the greens and blanch for 4–5 minutes, then drain. This step helps to reduce any bitterness in the greens but you can skip it.

3. Heat the oil in a wide, shallow frying pan. Add the garlic and cook over a high heat for 1 minute, until fragrant.

4. Add the leaves, water and lemon juice. Bring to the boil and cook over a medium-low heat 15 or up to 40 minutes, or until the leaves are done to your liking. Stir occasionally.

5. Stir and season with salt and pepper to taste. Serve as a side dish or over rice.

Adi's cauli–jadara

Rice and brown lentil mujadara with caramelised cauliflower

Mujadara is a tasty Middle Eastern staple, made with golden caramelised onions mixed with lentils and rice or bulgur wheat (depending on the location). Like many great dishes, it was considered poor man's food: a way to transform cheap ingredients into a wholesome meal.

This take on *mujadara* was created by my wife, Adi. She told me that after all the months of testing my cauliflower experiments, she decided to try a creation on me – and boy, was that a success!

Later that day we invited friends for dinner. One of them does not like onion, in any shape or form, so he was also pleased with Adi's creation, now officially named cauli-jadara.

Feel free to play around with the spice combo in the recipe: I used cumin, but turmeric, coriander seeds and even ground allspice work well.

serves 4–5 / vegan / gluten-free /
prep and cook: 40 minutes, plus soaking time

Ingredients

For the rice and lentils

185 g (6½ oz/1 cup) green or brown lentils, soaked in plenty
 of water for 2 hours
200 g (7 oz/1 cup) basmati rice, well rinsed and drained
3 tablespoons olive oil
1/2 teaspoon ground cumin (or more to taste)
750 ml (5 fl oz/3 cups) water
1 scant teaspoon fine sea salt (or more to taste)

For the caramelised cauliflower

1 medium-small cauliflower
1/2 teaspoons sea salt
80 ml (3 fl oz/⅓ cup) olive oil

Method

1. **To cook the rice and lentils:** Strain the lentils and transfer to a medium-size saucepan with the rice.

2. Add the oil and cumin, stir and cover with the water (it should cover the ingredients by 2 cm (¾ in). Bring to the boil and season with salt (the water should be a bit salty).

3. Cover the pan and cook over a very low heat for about 20 minutes or until the rice and lentils have absorbed all the water. Remove from the heat and leave to rest for 20 minutes.

4. **For the caramelised cauliflower:** Cut the cauliflower into florets, then chop them finely into small pieces that resemble breadcrumbs (or use a food processor or box grater). Move the cauliflower pieces to a wide pan and add the salt and oil. Cook over medium-high heat, stirring, 10–14 minutes until golden but not brown.

5. Empty the pan with the caramelised cauliflower, including the oil, into the rice and lentil pan. Gently stir to combine but be careful not to break the rice.

6. The cauli-jadara keeps for 3 days in the fridge and can be frozen for up to 1 month.

Cauliflower and red lentil kichri
Cauliflower rice taken to the next level

Kichri is an Iraqi dish with Indian roots made with rice and red lentils. The Indian dish (also named *khichdi*) is rich with spices, herbs and even nuts, whereas the Iraqi version is more minimal in nature.

Due to its nutritional value, *kichri* is prepared by some Jews of Iraqi descent before ritual fasting. The final step of preparation is what makes it unique: garlic and cumin are fried in oil and drizzled on top of the dish.

In this recipe I make *kichri* just like my grandmother, Hanna, taught me, but use cauliflower grains instead of rice. After seeing them do so well in stir-fried 'rice' (see page 138), I wanted to test their power in a different rice dish, and I am very proud of the results.

The amount of water I use might not seem like much, but it is enough because you only need moisture for the lentils. If you put too much water, things will get mushy.

You can top your *kichri* with fried eggs, baked or fried aubergines (eggplants), grated fresh tomatoes, sour cream and chopped spring onions (scallions).

serves 4–5 / vegan (omit yoghurt) / prep and cook: 1 hour

Ingredients

For the cauliflower and lentils

1 medium-size cauliflower
250 g (9 oz/1 cup) red lentils, preferably whole
2–3 tablespoons olive oil
1 scant teaspoon ground turmeric
350 ml (12 fl oz/1½ cups) water
fine sea salt

To finish the dish

6–7 garlic cloves, peeled and grated
3–6 tablespoons olive oil
1 teaspoon ground cumin (or whole seeds)
natural yoghurt, homemade tahini (see page 38) or lemon
  wedges, to serve

Method

1. **To cook the cauliflower and lentils:** Cut the cauliflower into florets. Chop the florets into small pieces that resemble breadcrumbs (using a food processor, a box grater or a knife). Place the lentils in a fine sieve and rinse really well (stirring with your hands). Allow to drain.

2. Place the cauliflower crumbs and lentils in a medium-size saucepan. Add the oil, turmeric and water, and stir.

3. Bring to the boil over a high heat, season generously with salt, cover, reduce the heat to low and cook for 12–16 minutes, until the cauliflower and lentils are tender but not mushy.

4. **To finish:** Place the garlic and oil in a small frying pan over a medium heat and cook for 20–30 seconds until fragrant.

5. Add the cumin and fry for a further 20–30 seconds until the aromas are deeply satisfying. If you see the garlic beginning to take colour, remove from the heat.

6. Empty the pan with the sizzling garlic and cumin into the cauliflower and lentils. Combine gently. Serve alongside yoghurt, tahini or with a wedge of lemon.

Cauliflower and spinach shakshooka
Who needs tomatoes?

Shakshooka, a breakfast dish of eggs cooked in spicy tomato sauce is popular in Israel, Libya and Tunisia. Over time, Israeli cooks got creative, and *shakshooka* started describing various other dishes of eggs cooked in vegetable-based sauces – most famous of which is the green *shakshooka*, that contains spinach.

The idea to upgrade green *shakshooka* came from my fellow Israeli food blogger Hagit Bilia.

I was telling Hagit about my grand plans for the white princess, and she asked me: 'Why don't you make a cauliflower *shakshooka* with spinach and some good cheese?'. 'That will work!', I replied, and very soon after she posted a very luscious *shakshooka* on her blog, proving the feasibility of the concept in the most delicious way possible.

serves 3–5 / contains eggs and dairy / gluten-free / paleo / prep and cook: 30 minutes

Ingredients

1 small cauliflower
4 tablespoons olive oil
60 ml (2 fl oz/¼ cup) water
500 g (1 lb 2 oz) fresh spinach leaves, rinsed and roughly chopped if large
sea salt and freshly ground black pepper
6–8 medium to large eggs, preferably free-range
60 g (2 oz) feta or chèvre cheese, to serve (optional)
slices of good bread, to serve

Method

1. Cut the cauliflower into florets, then thinly slice (reserve the other parts for stock, see page 22).

2. Heat the olive oil in a wide, shallow frying pan. Add the sliced cauliflower and sauté over a high heat for 6–7 minutes, stirring frequently, until just tender and golden.

3. Add the water, bring to the boil, cover and cook over a medium-high heat for a further 5 minutes until tender. Add the chopped spinach and stir well. Cook for 3 minutes, stirring occasionally, until the leaves have wilted and lost most of their volume.

4. If you see too much water pooling in the bottom of the pan, push all the vegetables to one side, then allow the excess liquid to reduce (3–5 minutes over a high heat).

5. Stir well and, using a spoon, create little holes in the cauli-spinach mixture (according to the number of eggs you are using). Crack the eggs into the holes.

6. Cover the pan and cook over a medium heat for 5–8 minutes until the eggs are done to your liking.

7. Crumble over the feta, if using, and serve alongside some chunks of good bread.

Cauliflower and aubergine maqluba
Upside-down rice cake

Maqluba, literally meaning upside down, is one of the most glorious rice dishes around: a spectacular dish composed of crispy rice, fried vegetables, chicken and spices, that is turned upside down when served to present its beauty to the fortunate diners.

Cauliflower and aubergine (eggplant) are often common ingredients in a traditional Arab Maqluba, but not the main ones. Here they take centre stage.

Aubergine is known as the king of vegetables in Israel, so it is only fitting to match him with our white queen. All parts of the cauliflower are used here.

Do pick fresh aubergines that feel light for their size. Old and heavy ones tend to be more bitter.

serves 6 / vegan / prep and cook: 2 hours

Ingredients
400 g (4 oz/2 cups) long-grain white rice
1 medium-size aubergine (eggplant)
80 ml (3 fl oz/⅓ cup) olive oil
1 medium-small cauliflower
1 teaspoon ground turmeric
1 teaspoon paprika (hot, sweet or smoked, to your liking)
850 ml (29 fl oz/3½ cups) water (or, even better –
  Cauliflower Stock! See page 22)
fine sea salt and freshly ground black pepper

Method

1. Preheat the oven to 190°C (375°F/Gas 5).

2. Place the rice in a bowl, cover with water and soak for 1 hour.

3. **To cook the aubergine:** Slice the aubergine (eggplant) into 1½ cm (½ in) thick rounds. Drizzle 3 tablespoons oil onto a baking tray (baking sheet) lined with parchment paper. Dip each slice in the oil, on both sides, and arrange them evenly spaced on the sheet. Season with salt and bake for 22–25 minutes until golden and soft.

4. **To cook the cauliflower:** Cut off the cauliflower florets. Peel and dice the main stem into medium cubes. Finely chop the stalks and leaves.

5. Heat 3–4 tablespoons of oil in a wide frying pan over a high heat. Place one layer of florets cut-side down and sear for 2–3 minutes or until lightly golden on one side. Transfer to a plate or bowl and repeat with remaining florets (see picture opposite).

6. In the same pan (still over a high heat), add the chopped stalks and diced stem, and sauté for 4–6 minutes until just tender.

7. **For the rice:** Strain the rice and drain well. Move to a large bowl, add the sautéed cauliflower parts, turmeric and paprika, and stir to combine. Season with salt and pepper (see picture overleaf).

To assemble: Lay one layer of seared florets, seared-side down, at the bottom of a medium-size non-stick pan. Top with ⅓ of the rice mixture. Arrange the remaining florets on top and spread with another one-third of the rice mixture. Layer the baked aubergine rounds on top and cover with the remaining rice (see picture overleaf). Pour over the water (or stock) and bring to the boil over high heat. Season generously with salt (the liquid should be salty).

8. Cover the pan and cook over low heat for 20 minutes until the rice is fully cooked. Some aubergine slices might float to the surface and that's okay. Remove the pan from the heat and allow to rest for at least 40 minutes.

9. When ready to serve, shake the pan from side to side to release the rice. Lay a plate over the pot, turn over decisively and serve. Leftovers keep refrigerated for 4 days.

As a safety measure for successful turnover, cut some parchment paper to a round that fits in the bottom of pan, and place it there before assembling.

Cauli**tip**

Tal's cauliflower risotto
Made with just a single cauliflower

Every year, my younger sister, Tal, asks me to make a special dish for her birthday. Four years ago, she said she dreamt of a cauliflower risotto. I know that is not a typical request, but I have been making risottos for my family since I started cooking professionally.

One chef that I have always admired is Gordon Ramsay (I even translated one of his cookbooks into Hebrew). Based on his risotto recipe I developed the cauli-version for Tal's birthday dinner.

This dish summarises the book well: it contains three elements: stock, cream and fried florets, utilising every part of a single magnificent cauliflower. It received much praise from my family.

A classic risotto should include Parmesan cheese and butter, but this dish is so good you can easily make it totally dairy-free (and no one will notice).

serves 3–4 / contains dairy / prep and cook: 1½ hours

Ingredients

For the cream and stock

1 medium-large cauliflower, with outer stalks intact
1 litre (40 fl oz/5 cups) water, for the stock
750–950 ml (26–32 fl oz/3–4 cups) water, for the cream
40 g (1½ oz) butter or 60 ml (2 fl oz/¼ cup) coconut cream
sea salt, to taste

For the risotto

3 tablespoons olive oil
1 medium onion, peeled or 1 leek, rinsed and finely chopped
300 g (12 oz/1½ cups) risotto rice, such as Arborio, carnaroli, or vialone nano
120 ml (4 fl oz/½ cup) dry or semi-dry white wine (use one you will drink)
oil, for deep-frying (see Caulitip)
10 chive sprigs or 2 spring onions (scallions), finely chopped
sea salt and cracked white pepper

Method

1. **To make the cauliflower stock:** Cut the cauliflower into florets and set them aside. Roughly chop the stalks and stem and put them in a medium-sized saucepan with the water for the stock. Bring to the boil over a high heat. Add any stock-worthy vegetable parts to hand.

2. Cover and cook over a medium heat for 20 minutes until the water is infused with a delicate cauliflower flavour. Season with about 1 teaspoon of salt and keep the pan simmering.

3. **To make the cream:** Cut half of the florets into bite-size pieces and place in a small saucepan with enough of the water for the cream to just cover the florets. Cook, uncovered, over a medium heat for 16 minutes until the florets are completely tender.

4. Remove about 240 ml (8 fl oz/1 cup) of the cooking liquid and set aside. Add the butter or coconut cream and purée, using a hand-held blender until you reach a very smooth, creamy consistency. Season with salt to taste.

5. **To make the risotto base:** Heat the oil in a wide shallow saucepan. Add the chopped onion or leek and sweat over a medium heat for 5 minutes until just tender, stirring occasionally.

6. Add the rice and cook for 1 minute. Add the wine, bring to the boil and allow it to evaporate. When the pan appears almost dry, start ladling in the hot stock, 2 ladlefuls at a time, stirring well every 1–2 minutes. Cook over a medium heat, keeping the liquid bubbling constantly. When all of the liquid has been absorbed into the rice, add 2 more ladlefuls of stock. Continue in this way twice more, by which time the rice should feel tender on the outside and a bit firm inside (continue cooking if not).

7. **To cook the fried florets:** Meanwhile, cut the remaining florets into small (walnut-size) pieces. Heat the oil for deep-frying in a small saucepan. Fry the florets in 2–3 batches for 3–4 minutes until golden. Transfer to kitchen paper and season lightly with salt.

8. **To finish:** When the rice is almost done, add about one-third of the cream and most of the chives then stir well. Remove the pan from the heat, and season with salt and pepper. Add more cream for a richer risotto (see picture below).

9. To serve, divide between serving plates and top each with fried florets and remaining chives.

To bake the florets, place them in a pan lined with greaseproof paper. Drizzle with 3–4 tablespoons of oil, toss and roast in an oven preheated to 190°C (375°F/Gas 5) for 15–20 minutes, or until golden and tender.

Caulitip

Cauliflower paella
With peas and smoked paprika

Paella is one of the national dishes of Spain, originating from the Andalusia region. Like the French cassoulet and Moroccan tajine, the dish is named after the pan: a very shallow wide one, to be precise.

Traditionally rice, saffron, seafood, chorizo and various vegetables cook together in the paella pan, which is set over an open fire outdoors. The peak of the dish is its bottom: Spaniards claim the caramelised rice that is closest to the heat is worth fighting over.

I'm not suggesting you start a bonfire or even buy a paella pan, necessarily. I do, suggest you embrace the easy-to-master technique, using any shallow, wide pan you might have at hand.

In this vegetable-based paella, cauliflower is used three times: cauliflower stock is the liquid that gives it depth, the stalks add some texture and aroma, and seared florets are the main attraction on top.

serves 4 / vegan / prep and cook: 1 hour

Ingredients

1 small cauliflower, with outer stalks in tact
3–4 ripe medium-size tomatoes
6–9 tablespoons olive oil
1 medium-size onion, peeled and diced into small cubes
1 red bell pepper, diced into small cubes
4–6 garlic cloves, peeled and thinly sliced
300 g (12 oz/1½ cups) paella or risotto rice, such as Arborio, carnaroli, or vialone nano
1 teaspoon smoked paprika
a small pinch of saffron strands (optional)
750 ml–1 litre (25–34 fl oz/3–4 cups) warm Cauliflower Stock (see page 22)
large handful of frozen peas
handful of parsley leaves, chopped, to garnish
sea salt and freshly ground black pepper

Method

1. Cut the cauliflower into florets. Cut each floret into 4–6 wedges. Rinse well and finely chop three nice cauliflower stalks. You can add the remaining stalks to the pan of warm stock standing by.

2. Grate the tomatoes into a bowl.

3. **To sear the florets:** Heat a wide, shallow pan over your widest burner. Add 3 tablespoons of oil and lay a single layer of cauliflower wedges in the oil. Sear over a medium–high heat for 2–4 minutes on each side, until lightly golden. Remove to a plate and sear the remaining wedges in the same way, adding more oil if needed.

4. **To make the paella:** Add the remaining oil to the pan. Add the onion, pepper and chopped cauliflower stalks and sauté over a medium–high heat for 3–4 minutes until just tender (see picture overleaf).

5. Add the garlic, rice, paprika and saffron (if using). Cook for 1 minute, stirring.

6. Add the grated tomatoes and 500 ml (16 fl oz/2 cups) of warm stock. Stir well and season with salt and pepper.

7. Return the seared cauliflower to the pan and stir gently. Bring to the boil, cover, and cook over a medium heat for 10 minutes until the rice has absorbed most of the liquid.

8. Add the frozen peas and gently stir them in. If you see any dry areas, ladle them with the stock (see picture overleaf).

9. Cook for a further 5–15 minutes, uncovered, ladling the stock over dry areas as you go. The paella is ready when the rice is tender and there is a lovely golden-brown layer at the bottom of the pan (see picture below).

10. Serve at once to the centre of the table, garnished with chopped parsley if you like.

 For extra freshness, serve the paella with a green salsa (see page 58).

Caulitip

Iraqi-style meatballs
Braised with cauliflower, garlic and mint

One of my grandmother's signature dishes is *koobah* (also known as *kibbeh* or *kubbeh*): semolina dumplings filled with meat and herbs, cooked in a sweet-sour soup.

During the spring, in the short season of green garlic, she cooks her dumplings in a sauce called *thumiyeh*, which contains an outrageous amount of garlic, fresh mint and lemon juice

I would need at least 20 pages to explain how to master *koobah*, so here is a short cut: I turned my grandmother's filling into meatballs, and added a head of cauliflower to the tasty braising liquid. The florets have a crumbly texture, echoing that of the typical semolina casing.

The Middle Eastern spice blend *baharat* is used to give the meatballs their distinct flavour. Among its' typical ingredients you will find: nutmeg, dried ginger, allspice, cinnamon, black pepper and cloves.

Iraqi *baharat* also features dried rose petals and dried cardamom. You can buy it in Middle Eastern stores and order online.

serves 5 / contains meat / prep and cook: 1 hour

Ingredients

For the sauce

1 small cauliflower
3–4 tablespoons olive oil
1 medium-size onion, peeled and diced into cubes
cloves from 3–4 heads of garlic, peeled
leaves from 15–30 mint sprigs (the more, the merrier)
3–4 tablespoons wheat semolina
700–980 ml (24–30 fl oz/3–4 cups) water
5 tablespoons freshly squeezed lemon juice
sea salt
1 tablespoon brown/white sugar (or more to taste)

For the meatballs

1 medium-size onion, peeled
about 75 g (2½ oz/small bunch) parsley (use everything including the stems)
500 g (1 lb 2 oz) minced beef
1 tablespoon baharat
1 large egg, preferably free-range
4–5 tablespoons wheat semolina
1 teaspoon fine sea salt
oil, for shallow-frying (optional)
steamed rice, to serve

Method

1. **For the sauce:** Cut the cauliflower into medium-size florets (you can also add its other parts: stem, peeled and chopped, stalks chopped).

2. Heat the oil in a wide shallow pan. Add the onions and sauté over a high heat for 7–9 minutes, until lightly golden. Add the florets (and other parts, if using), garlic cloves, most of the mint leaves, the semolina and the water and bring to the boil (see picture overleaf).

3. Add the lemon juice and season with salt and sugar to taste. Simmer the sauce over a low heat while you get working on the meatballs.

4. **To make the meatballs:** Grate the onion into a bowl using a box grater. Squeeze and discard excess water. Finely chop the parsley.

5. Place the minced beef in a large bowl and knead with your hands for 2–3 minutes until it feels smoother. Add the grated squeezed onion, chopped parsley, baharat, egg and semolina. Season with the salt and mix to combine.

6. Using wet hands, form the mixture to ping-pong size balls. If you wish to fry the meatballs first, heat the oil for shallow-frying in a medium-size frying pan. Fry the meatballs in batches for 2 minutes on each side until golden.

7. Gently lay the meatballs in the sauce and simmer, uncovered, for 20–30 minutes until the meatballs are tender and juicy, and the sauce has reduced by half. Taste and add more salt, sugar or lemon juice to your liking. Stir in the remaining mint leaves (see picture below).

8. Serve with rice.

9. The braised meatballs keep refrigerated for 4 days, and taste even better after a night in the fridge.

Gluten-free: Replace the wheat semolina with polenta.

Vegan: See the vegan appendix to the book online – https://goo.gl/ndJp7m.

Caulitip

Inside-out stuffed cauliflower
With Swiss chard and preserved lemon

In the previous recipe, the cauliflower was with the meatballs, now it goes to the next level, merging with the balls themselves. The inner stem pops out like a lamb chop, and when you cut it through you see the white floret in all its glory.

By now, you must have noticed my tendency to make the most of the vegetables at my disposal, and this dish is no exception. I use both green and white parts of the earthy Swiss chard: the white fibrous stalk is used at the start of the recipe, while the green leaves are added at later to create textural complexity.

Note that you can cook the stuffed cauliflower in any other sauce you like.

serves 4–5 / contains meat / prep and cook: 1 1/2 hours

Ingredients

For the stuffed cauliflower

500–600 g (1¼ lb) minced beef
leaves from 6–8 mint sprigs
about 75 g (2½ oz/small bunch) parsley (including the stems)
1 large egg, preferably free-range
4–5 heaped tablespoons breadcrumbs
sea salt and freshly ground black pepper
1 small cauliflower
oil, for shallow-frying (optional)
steamed rice, to serve

For the sauce

1 bunch Swiss chard (containing 5–6 large leaves)
2–3 tablespoons olive oil
1 tablespoon finely chopped preserved lemons (from about 1–2 lemons)
1/2 teaspoon ground turmeric
3–4 tablespoons freshly squeezed lemon juice
1 heaped tablespoon wheat semolina
750–975 ml (26–33 fl oz/3–4 cups) water
1 tablespoon brown sugar (or more to taste, whatever kind you have)

Method

1. **To make the meat mixture:** Place the minced beef in a large bowl and knead with your hands for 2–3 minutes until it feels smoother. Add the herbs, egg and breadcrumbs. Season well with salt and pepper and mix to combine.

2. Cut the cauliflower into medium-sized florets. Cut the larger florets, from the bottom of the head, into quarters lengthways.

3. Using wet hands, divide the beef mixture into balls – one ball for each floret standing by. Push the florets into the balls, then tightly wrap, allowing the stem to pop out (see pictures opposite and overleaf).

4. **To fry:** If you wish to brown the meatballs, heat the oil in a medium-sized frying pan. Fry the coated florets, in batches, for 2 minutes on each side until golden brown.

5. **To make the sauce**: Separate the white stalks from the leafy Swiss chard leaves. Dice the stalks; shred the leaves into 1 cm (½ in) wide strips.

6. Heat the oil in a wide shallow frying pan. Add the stalks and sauté over a high heat for 5 minutes until just tender.

7. Add half the leaves, the preserved lemon, turmeric, lemon juice, semolina (our thickening agent) and water. Season with salt and sugar, and bring to the boil.

8. Gently lay the wrapped florets in the sauce and simmer, uncovered, for 20–40 minutes until the coating is tender and juicy and the sauce has reduced by half.

9. Taste and add more salt, sugar or lemon juice to your liking, stir in the remaining Swiss chard leaves and cook for a final 3–4 minutes, until just wilted.

10. Serve, alongside rice. The dish keeps refrigerated for up to 4 days, and tastes even better after a night in the fridge.

Paleo: Omit the semolina and sugar, replace the breadcrumbs with a potato, grated and squeezed.

Gluten-free: Replace wheat semolina with polenta.

Vegan: See the vegan appendix to the book online – https://goo.gl/ndJp7m.

Caulitip

You can omit the preserved lemon, adding 2–3 tablespoons of lemon juice instead.

Giant cauliflower mafrum

Libyan-style whole stuffed cauliflower with beef and herbs

Mafrum is one of the most loved Libyan dishes in Israel. It was brought here with the mass return of Jews from Tripoli after 1948. The word mafrum often describes slices of stuffed aubergine (eggplant) or potatoes cooked in a tomato-purée-based sauce, served over fluffy couscous. It's a treat.

Some home cooks make cauliflower *mafrums*, which led to the ambitious idea presented here. It is based on an authentic recipe given to me by Orna Ban Haim – a PR woman and talented home cook.

She invited me to her kitchen and taught me all the steps of her family recipe. I adapted it to a whole cauliflower and the results are as mouthwatering as they are impressive. Many readers have reported that this *mafrum* was a huge success in their homes.

serves 4–5 / contains meat / prep and cook: 2 hours

Ingredients

For the filling

about 75 g (2½ oz/small bunch) parsley (including the stems)
2 slices of bread (plain white works, challah bread is better)
500 g (1 lb 2 oz) minced beef
1 medium potato, grated and squeezed of excess moisture
¼ teaspoon ground cinnamon
sea salt and freshly ground black pepper
2 medium-size eggs, preferably free-range

For the cauliflower

1 medium-size cauliflower, with outer stalks in tact
60 g (2 oz/½ cup) plain (all-purpose) flour
1 medium-size egg, preferably free-range
6 tablespoons olive oil

For the sauce

3–4 tablespoons olive oil
1 large onion, peeled and diced into cubes
3–4 garlic cloves, peeled and minced or finely chopped
4 tablespoons tomato purée (paste)
500–750 ml (16–24 fl oz/2–3 cups) water
½ teaspoon ground cinnamon
½ tablespoon brown sugar (to taste)
1 teaspoon sweet paprika
fine sea salt and freshly ground black pepper
steamed couscous or rice, to serve

Method

1. Preheat the oven to 190°C (375°F/Gas 5).

2. **To make the filling:** Finely chop the parsley. Soak the bread in water for 2 minutes, then drain and squeeze out the excess. Place the bread and squeezed grated potato in a large bowl and add the minced beef, parsley, cinnamon and season with salt and pepper. Mix well to combine.

3. Crack in the eggs and knead for 2 minutes, or until the mix feels smoother. Cover with cling film (plastic wrap) and refrigerate while you get on with the remaining recipe.

4. **To cook the cauliflower:** Remove all the cauliflower stalks, reserving 2–3 aside for the sauce. Steam the cauliflower whole (see page 24) for 15 minutes or until tender. Remove from the saucepan and let the cauliflower cool down for 10 minutes.

5. **To make the sauce:** Finely chop the reserved cauliflower stalks. Heat the oil in a pan large enough to fit the cauliflower whole. Add the stalks and onion and sauté over a high heat for 5–6 minutes until just tender.

6. Add the garlic and tomato purée (paste) and cook over a medium heat for 1 minute. Add ⅔ of the water, the cinnamon, sugar and paprika and stir well. Bring to the boil and season with salt and pepper to taste.

7. Cover and simmer over a low heat for 30–40 minutes, until the flavours come together. Add more water if you see things drying up.

8. **To fill the cauliflower:** Hold the cauliflower upside-down. Push the meat mixture between the inner stems to fill the gaps. Turn over and gently separate the florets (without disconnecting them from the main stem). Fill these gaps with the meat mixture (see picture overleaf).

9. **To bake and cook the stuffed cauliflower:** Place the flour on a shallow plate. Beat the egg in a shallow bowl. Coat the cauliflower with flour, shake off excess and coat with the egg (see picture overleaf).

10. Drizzle 2 tablespoons of oil in a wide, shallow non-stick roasting pan or ovenproof dish. Place the cauliflower in the pan and drizzle the remaining 4 tablespoons of oil on top. Bake for 25–30 minutes until nicely golden throughout (see picture overleaf).

11. Using a sturdy metal spatula, carefully lift the baked cauliflower and place in the sauce. The sauce should reach halfway up the cauliflower – add more water if needed.

12. Bring to the boil, cover and simmer over a medium-low heat for 40–50 minutes, until the filling is fully cooked. Serve with couscous or rice. Keeps refrigerated for up to 4 days.

Gluten-free: Replace the bread with another grated potato; coat the cauliflower in gluten-free flour.

Vegan: See the vegan appendix to the book online – https://goo.gl/ndJp7m.

Cauli**tip**

INDEX

A note from the author

I don't talk a lot about my childhood, because it is a part of my life I'd rather suppress. Up to the beginning of high school, all through elementary and middle school, I was the fat nerd of the class, the one who was ridiculed, laughed at and boycotted.

I was the kid that took and absorbed the beatings and insults, the one who was easiest to pick on. There were days I would come back home crying from the threats of the thugs in my classes, and there were times I just wanted to stay home because of how bad I felt. Someone I met, who went to elementary school with me, used these words: 'they gave you hell'.

Deep inside I am still that kid who just wants everyone to feel good and be happy, and doesn't understand what he did wrong. That period of my life left me with a lot of pain, and during the following years, in the process of maturing and healing myself, a deep, powerful urge to succeed was embedded in me.

The entire process of crowd-funding the publishing of this book (in Hebrew), which required relentless determination and perseverance, felt like the emendation of my childhood days. There is nothing more satisfying than seeing people you have never met pledge and rally for you and your idea, willing to invest their money and time to make someone else's dream come true.

About ten years ago I met a yoga master, who analysed my chakras (centres of energy in the body, according to Hindu faith). He told me that my heart chakra, the one associated with compassion, giving and love, was closed shut. His words made me realise I was not spending enough time doing the things I love. That's how I slowly moved in to the world of food, dedicating myself to cooking and feeding my family, writing and sharing the knowledge and experience I gained.

The kitchen is where my heart is happy, and so I hope this book will be of constant use in your kitchen. May the dishes and recipes become permanent residents on your dining table, may you be inspired to invent new dishes of your own, and mostly, may you create many moments of happiness using the words and pictures found within these pages.

With plenty of love, Oz Telem

Acknowledgements

The book you are now holding is the realisation of a dream I've had since my early days of cooking. It came to be in a non-traditional way of crowd-funding. Over 750 people supported, purchased and backed the book while it was merely an idea and a promise: loyal readers and followers, friends and colleague, family and complete strangers.

First, I would like to thank my family for pushing, supporting and believing in me all the way, and to my wife, Adi, and her family for their belief and kind words.

I would like to thank my 'team cauliflower', who took my vision and turned it to a delicious reality:

To Raheli, my editor and mentor, who guided and helped nurture the idea from day one.

To Assaf, the photographer, who, with great dedication, documented even the smallest of steps.

To Noa, the food stylist, who succeeded in making every picture tell its own story.

To Dan, the designer, who combined the text and pictures in the most synergetic way.

And to Sima and Kobi, the Israeli printers, who advised and supported the entire process.

I would also like to extend my gratitude to Esti, who joined in at the final stretch to hone and polish the recipes, to Eli, our video master, and to Gill from Farma Cultura farm.

To all those who joined to support and back my project, shared, commented and empowered me through the journey: I could not have done this without you.

I also wish to thank the dozens of recipe testers, who volunteered to try out the recipes before publishing, and whose feedback proved vital.

Lastly, I want to thank Kate, Stephen, Kajal, Molly, Eila and all the good people at Hardie Grant Publishing, for believing in the cauliflower (and in me), and allowing the book to be translated and published in the English language.

And a special gratitude to Margaux who, nine years ago, got an email from an anonymous young man from Israel, who told her he wished to translate Gordon Ramsay into Hebrew, and replied: why not? Neither would have guessed they would once again cross paths, this time in the way of the cauliflower.

Cauliflower by Oz Telem

First published by Oz Telem
This English edition published in 2018 by Hardie Grant Books,
an imprint of Hardie Grant Publishing

Hardie Grant Books (London)
5th and 6th Floors
52–54 Southwark Street
London SE1 1UN

Hardie Grant Books (Melbourne)
Building 1, 658 Church Street
Richmond, Victoria 3121

hardiegrantbooks.com

All rights reserved. No part of this publication may be reproduced,
stored in a retrieval system or transmitted in any form by any
means, electronic, electrostatic, magnetic tape, mechanical,
photocopying, recording or otherwise, without the prior written
permission of the Publisher.

The moral rights of the author have been asserted.

Text© Oz Telem

Photography© Assaf Ambram

British Library Cataloguing-in-Publication Data. A catalogue record
for this book is available from the British Library.

ISBN: 978-1-78488-178-8

Publisher: Kate Pollard
Senior Editor: Molly Ahuja
Publishing Assistant: Eila Purvis
Food stylist: Noa Kanarek
Hebrew edition designer: Dan Kopman
Translator: Oz Telem
English copyeditor: Wendy Hobson
English proofreader: Kate Wanwimolruk
English typesetter: David Meikle
English design: p2d
English indexer: Cathy Heath
English colour reproduction by p2d

Printed and bound in China by Toppan Leefung Printing Ltd.